Theodor Hertzka

A visit to Freeland

The new paradise regained

Theodor Hertzka

A visit to Freeland
The new paradise regained

ISBN/EAN: 9783743463479

Manufactured in Europe, USA, Canada, Australia, Japa

Cover: Foto ©Andreas Hilbeck / pixelio.de

Manufactured and distributed by brebook publishing software (www.brebook.com)

Theodor Hertzka

A visit to Freeland

A VISIT TO FREELAND.

Bellamy Library, No. 21.

A VISIT TO FREELAND,

OR

THE NEW PARADISE REGAINED,

BY

DR. THEODOR HERTZKA,

*Author of "Freeland," "The Laws of Social Development," etc.,
President of the International Freeland Society.*

London:

WILLIAM REEVES, 185, FLEET STREET, E.C.,
AND
BRITISH FREELAND ASSOCIATION, 107, QUEEN VICTORIA ST., E.C.

CONTENTS.

                                                                    PAGE.
Chapter I.
Why I Went 1

Chapter II.
The Journey 11

Chapter III.
Where Freeland is situated, and what it is ... 18

Chapter IV.
Who cleaned my boots in Freeland, the Appearance of the Streets and the Ownership of Dwelling Houses 24

Chapter V.
How I chose a Business in Freeland, and paid for my Dinner at the Restaurant 33

Chapter VI.
The Constitution of a Manufacturing Company in Freeland, and the Profit obtained from it ... ...

Chapter VII.
Why Freeland uses so much Machinery and whence obtains it ... ...

CONTENTS.

CHAPTER VIII.
A Household in Freeland and the Right of Main

CHAPTER IX.
The Central Bank—The Monetary System—The Central Warehouse—Freedom in Freeland ... ...

CHAPTER X.
Impossibility of a Crisis in Freeland—The Insurance System 90

CHAPTER XI.
A Holiday Journey in Freeland—Distribution of Land and Capital ... ... ͤ

CHAPTER XII.
Founding a New Company in Freeland 113

CHAPTER XIII.
The Constitution and Taxation of Freeland 122

CHAPTER XIV.
Society, Love and Religion in Freeland 132

CHAPTER XV.
Fitness of the Professions which People choose—Art Productions — Communism and Anarchism — The Administration—General Practicability of the Fundamental Principles of Freeland—Fear of Overpopulation 142

CHAPTER XVI.
clusion 154

PREFACE.

In the first place, I confess that this little book is written with an object in the fullest sense of the word. It desires not only to bring the reader over to its opinions under the veil of amusement and instruction, but also to induce him to coöperate in a more practical sense. Not only does it make designs on his mind and heart, but also on his purse and resolutions.

The majority of those who read this passage may indeed say with a smile of superiority that the altogether too conscientious author might have spared this warning. Dispositions as well as purses are too well guarded nowadays for any obtrusive object to be able to succeed easily in taking possession of them. If I add that the undertaking for which, by means of this work, I desire to win energetic coöperation, is neither more nor less than the creation of a Community based on social liberty and justice, that is, one that will guarantee to everybody the full and entire produce of his own work by the unlimited maintenance of his right of doing what he pleases, the supercilious smile will be slightly mixed with compassion, and when I confess besides that this El Dorado is situated in the Highlands of Africa and just on the equator, there are probably few who would suppose that they could accept such exaggerated fancies in earnest without causing serious doubts as to their education, their sound common sense, and even their sanity. "Let the author be content," I hear some say; "we read Utopias of this kind if they are made entertaining. They do to pass away an idle hour, and that is all."

But the reader is mistaken! I speak from experience! This book is not the first that I have written for the same purpose. Four years ago I published a book called "Freeland: a Picture of Society in the Future," of which the reader has probably already heard some obscure report. The nine German editions which have hitherto been published, and numerous others in foreign languages, enticed thousands and hundreds of thousands of men and women of all conditions in all parts of the inhabited world, from the prince himself to the simple workman, to the determination to carry into execution what is described in it. Associations have been formed in twenty-eight European and American cities for the purpose of propagating the principles of Freeland. Money has been spent, a journal ("Freeland, Organ of the Freeland Society") has been started, lands on the east coast of Africa suitable for the foundation of places where the scheme is to be tried have been presented to the Society, and every preparation is being made to carry the great work into practice.

And what is the meaning of this unusual attempt to give effect to the vision contained in a book? It lies in the fact that this vision bears the stamp of the highest inner truth, that it can be literally realized if a sufficient number of energetic men, not quite destitute of means, should come together with this determination, and that what has for millenniums floated before the noblest minds as the goal of all their striving, thinking, and suffering, might be accomplished in this manner. The author of "Freeland" does not consider himself more wise, sagacious, or courageous than his great forerunners, since he will only give effect to what they longed for, but he shows that what has hitherto been impossible during the course of the development of the human race is now possible and even necessary, and why it is so. He maintains that "Freeland" is nothing else than the closing chapter of that great work of enlightenment for which the philanthropists of every generation have labored.

The exclusive intention of this little book is thus to get new helpers for this work of rescue. It conducts the reader to the Land of Liberty as if it already existed, in the hope that the institutions which he sees there will awaken in him the determination to contribute of his property to the quickest and most magnificent realization of a Commonwealth of Liberty and Justice. My above-mentioned work * describes in what manner this realization will come to pass, or rather, is already coming to pass, for the first pioneers of Freeland are actually on the way when "A Visit to Freeland" leaves the press. It need only be mentioned here that the outer scene and the inner working of the thoroughly simple events depicted in the following work correspond to the most sober truth in every detail. The Alpine landscapes of Kenia are, as a matter of fact, the paradise on earth that they are here represented to be, and the men whom I represent as there talking and acting, only talk and act, it is true, in my imagination, but all that they say and do follows the laws of the most sober necessity. Freeland is not founded at the time when I write this, but when it is founded, nothing else can really ever take place in it than what is related in "A Visit to Freeland."

Yet one thing more in conclusion. I have made a professor of political economy come upon the scene as a critic of the organization of Freeland, and have made some of the inhabitants refute his objections. It would appear as if a jester was brought forward in this guise to make as many self-evident mistakes as possible in order to help the cause of Freeland

---

* ' Freeland : a Social Anticipation." By Theodor Hertzka. Published by the British Freeland Association.

to an easy victory. But this is not the case. The professor does, indeed, exist only in the author's imagination, but, on the other hand, everything that he says must be read as if proceeding from the learned critics who have opposed my theories. In the preface of my above-mentioned earlier work, I had to subject every part of it to the severest test in consideration of the circumstance that it claimed to offer, in the form of a narrative, a picture of the actual future social state such as those learned in such subjects demand. This challenge was eagerly responded to by the specialists. Numerous articles have appeared in the daily papers, in journals devoted to social subjects, and in the form of pamphlets. Some of these agreed with "Freeland," while others blamed it; and what I now place in the mouth of Professor Tenax is nothing else but a flowery collection from the antagonistic reviews. At the same time I can certify here that I have not dealt with the worst, but with the best arguments which my antagonists employed. I have omitted nothing which might have a claim to regard either through the personal influence of the critic, or through the slightest appearance of internal validity, and I have likewise not admitted anything which did not demand notice for one of these reasons. I have not invented any of these criticisms, nor have I passed over any in silence, and if the impartial reader should find that the charges which Professor Tenax makes against the constitution of Freeland are calculated to demonstrate its impregnability in the clearest possible light, this will be a result for which I have not myself to thank, but my critics.

THEODOR HERTZKA.

VIENNA, 1894.

A Visit to Freeland.

CHAPTER I.

WHY I WENT.

NOTHING more detains me now. My determination is taken; I depart for Freeland.

And why do I undertake this journey? My friends say that it is because I am an eccentric dreamer: I even conjecture that they say shortly and simply when I am not present that it is because I am a fool. Perhaps they are right.

If having different opinions from everyone else upon all matters is called being foolish, then I am a fool, for my opinion upon every matter, at least upon every matter of importance, is different from that of my acquaintances and friends, of whom, since I am rich, I possess an astonishing large number, and they all think me fortunate—show me daily, with irrefutable arguments, that I am fortunate; whilst I, and this is my fixed idea, think myself very unfortunate. Not that I am a splenetic individual; heaven defend me from that. I am full of the impulse of life, and am by nature of a serene disposition. Besides that, I am young, have sound health, and, as I have already said, am rich. possess an agreeable personal appearance, and my success in society leaves so little to wish for that until a few hours ago I was the envied bridegroom of one of the most beautiful, most ...lished and most amiable maidens of one of the first ... of our town.

... sagacious reader here comes to the conclusion that

at the time when I write this I am no longer the bridegroom of this beautiful, accomplished, and amiable lady of good family, he will have guessed rightly. If he further concludes that perhaps it was this loss which made me feel so disgusted at the world, he is quite mistaken. The latter caused me to lose my bride, but my dismissal by her is quite innocent of the state of my feelings with regard to the world. On the contrary, I dare maintain that I feel quieter and more hopeful since he who would have been my father-in-law told me that I was an incorrigible silly fellow, who might for the future lay aside all idea of marrying his daughter; and the daughter, with tears in her eyes, but not on that account with less determination, gave her assent. But I must guard myself from the imputation that my bride was quite indifferent to me, and that only a bare match of convenience was bargained for between her and me, in which a position in society and suitable means were the most important consideration, and the persons only of secondary importance. But on the other hand—and on this point I never deceived myself—my external circumstances always formed the decision. My bride and all her family would have certainly not consented to a union with me, even were I a thousand times more prudent, handsome, and learned than I actually was, had I not possessed sufficient property besides. However, the reason why the engagement was broken off shows that even then they were not quite indifferent to my personal qualities, because the rupture was caused only in the manner that I have said, and was not in the least due to my worldly circumstances. And, besides, as far as my feelings are concerned, I can certify with a good conscience that they were always only influenced by the personal virtues and charms of my betrothed. I had never thought that my love was eternal, yet I would have declared anyone to be a black calumniator who had told me yesterday that I could renounce this radiantly beautiful creatu
As a matter of fact, the rupture of this engagement leave wonderfully indifferent, I even feel a rare satisfacti tranquillity on account of it. I feel as if I were fre a chain, and as if I were given back again to my self, and now for the first time both could and must

I should have done and really wished to do long ago, without being quite clear regarding the mode of doing it.

But with all this description, I have not yet said in what my misfortune, or what I think to be my misfortune, consists. It is, I am almost ashamed to confess, the misery which other people endure. I suffer because men, who do not specially concern me, are hungry and cold, and languish in want and degradation. I cannot get rid of the thought that it is my duty to help them somehow, notwithstanding the fact that they possess no other claim on my compassion than that they are, like me, born of women. And that is not merely a cold and careless idea which could easily be silenced by the belief that these miserable people will not allow anyone to help them, but a burning tempestuous desire which resists all attempts to lull it to sleep. The most delicate morsel becomes bitter if, on putting it into my mouth, I happen to think that my fellow men, whom I have since quite regarded in the light of equals, are in want of the barest necessaries, while I am gormandizing. At such a moment my morbid fancy conjures up all sorts of foolish ideas of hollow-eyed, languishing men, women, and children, and besides that I cannot help thinking that these very poor people are just those who must use the sweat of their brow and the marrow of their bones in producing that which I am about to enjoy. Then I seem to smell this sweat and to taste this marrow, and all comfortable enjoyment of the good things placed before me is of course gone. The same ideas occur to me with regard to all good and fine things which my riches allow me to possess, and which other men, who are not afflicted with any of these fancies, enjoy in peace. All these things torment me about my right to the lives of my deceived fellow men.

And if that were only all! But the tormenting demon in my disposition makes me answerable for all the vices and crimes of others. "That thief whom they have caught to-day," he whispers in my ear, "had never offended against the law if he had been allowed to feed himself and his family honorably. But you get the advantages of these laws. The robber and murderer who will be hanged to-morrow has committed his deed of violence out of sheer necessity. That girl at the street corner who sells her body for money would be a happy spouse and mother, if you had not hindered the lover of her choice from founding a family."

And so effective were these continual suggestions that the demon at last prevailed upon me to understand literally such expressions as "Love thy neighbor as thyself," "Do unto others what you would wish them to do to you," and to think about practising them; as if every cultured person did not know that they only exist that those of a susceptible disposition should edify themselves about the loftiness of their meaning, but not that any one should act according to them. What should we come to if we loved our neighbors as ourselves? We live in the age of humanity, and therefore do as much good to our neighbors as is reasonably possible. But the words "as thyself" mean "as a being of the same race and having the same right to life as ourselves, not as our domestic animals which we use up and deal with as mere means for our ends." Then, "Do unto others what you would wish to be done to yourself!" Can I be willing that others should use me for carrying their burdens? Certainly not. Therefore must I not forbear to use others for carrying my burdens?

To the horror of all my well minded friends, I am not alarmed by this very extreme consequence. Arguments which have stood the most severe tests were shattered to pieces by my infatuation That may answer to the ideal of justice— so they tell me—but if we all had to bear the burdens of the world equally, it would result in all of us being heavily laden, and all in poverty. This would not only be a bad exchange for the few who are in pleasant circumstances and impose their burdens on the multitude, but eventually for the multitude themselves. Universal poverty signifies the cessation of civilization, and a condition of barbarism. Civilization helps us to lighten the burdens of life; in other words, the workman of the civilized world is in a better condition than the savage.

And what do I answer to these most learned men who have the deepest insight into the connexion of all things? Am I moved by the self-denying humor of those noble people who entirely give themselves up, in the interests of the progress of civilization, to enjoy what is the result of the work of another? By no means. I ask, with diabolical scorn, for what purpose have we made all the magnificent discoveries of modern times of which we are so proud, if not for that of laying those burdens on the elements which we could not have supported alone by our own strength without detriment to the civilized world. Have we robbed the clouds of their lightning and the lower world of its fire merely that as much coal smoke as possible should ascend to the sky from numberless chimneys as a vapor offering? Perhaps that is the incense with which we fumigate our idol Mammon? For I have not hitherto been able to discover any other purpose in our so-called progress. The troubles of working men have not been lightened for an hour by the giants Steam and Electricity, but the misery of millions becomes more fierce and bitter the more our art of producing excess increases. And if humanity has become so silly as to consider all that as stable and unchangeable, this is a thoughtlessness from which former centuries and millenniums have been free. People have believed in former times as well as at present that misery and bondage are necessary, but they at least well knew why this should be so, and they had clear ideas as to what must happen in order that misery and bondage should be overcome. Plato and Aristotle said that bondage is founded on the incapacity to produce riches and ease for all. Aristotle said that if the weaver's shuttle could move without his aid and the plow without the aid of an ox, then all men would be free and equal. And the same opinion was expressed, only much more precisely, two thousand years later, by the great Bacon, Lord Verulam, the founder of modern natural philosophy. He prophesied the time when the elements would perform all coarse and hard work for man, and as a natural result of this that all bondage and misery would disappear from the world. Now the time has come when the weaver's shuttle moves without his aid, and the plow without the ox, and the elements are ready to perform all coarse and hard work for mankind, but the generation which experiences all this, and should be considered thrice happy if it knew what had fallen to its lot, shuts its eyes to the simple, reasonable enjoyment of measureless happiness, and still believing that bondage is necessary, condemns itself to misery.

But I certainly had, in spite of the demon, no clear idea as to how it was to be arranged so that every one could share in this happiness. I comprehended that the communistic and anarchistic world-improvement plans are not suitable. The one would turn the earth into a great compulsory workshop, the second at once surrender it to barbarism. I could spare neither liberty nor order; how to unite both, I knew not, however steadfast is my conviction that what must happen will happen.

But now the "Land of Liberty," the path of freedom and order, was founded, and I felt a strong inclination to walk in it. But my will was not strong enough to break the bonds which held me fast here. I should have been obliged to leave an old mother behind, and, when she was dead, a charming bride, and I had not the courage or power to leave either. But now I am free, free as a bird in the air, and that has happened in the following manner. One must not expect here any highly romantic disclosures. All that happened is as common as possible, and my broken off engagement would have been borne very differently by most people in my condition. But let us return to the matter in hand.

After all that I have already confessed to the reader, he will see clearly that living as a distinguished idler, as my wealth allowed me to, did not suit my disposition. Not that I imagined I could by means of some activity within the frame of society either cure or mitigate the misery which supported it. I wished to work earnestly because idleness appeared despicable to me. I chose, therefore, a business, that of engineer, and when my studies were ended, I solicited a suitable situation. That did not please the lady to whom I was engaged nor her parents, for they thought that another profession would have been more suitable for a young man of wealth and social rank if he really must work. In the meantime, as I held to my point, they let me do as I pleased.

But the appointment was delayed. Two years passed by, but the order appointing me did not come. Then the father of my bride interfered in the matter. I had certainly, as an unpractical idealist, which I really am, acted as perversely as possible; otherwise it is quite inconceivable that a man of my connexions would have had to wait so long a time for such a modest appointment. With regard to that I affirm that my connexions had nothing to do with my attempts to get the engagement. The manager with whom I had been discussing the matter knew nothing further about me, and as my family name is one of those which frequently come before the notice of the public, the worthy man did not in the least suppose that it was the rich and distinguished N. who would do him the honor to draw plans and construct machines under his guidance.

This conversation had taken place the day before yesterday. This morning an office servant brought the deed of my appointment to my house. Joyfully surprised, I hastily prepared to pay my visit of thanks to the manager. He received me with friendly reproofs because I sought for an appointment almost incognito, and apologized immediately for having made me wait so long. "If your future father-in-law had not honored me with a visit," he smilingly insinuated, "I should not have known to-day who you are."

I was not a little vexed with that. I had flattered myself that I should be able to obtain something through my testimonials, the proofs of my industry and knowledge, and now I saw myself brought into office through my connexions. But the thing was done, and so I made the best of a bad business. I took my leave with the usual courtesies, and only intended to reprove my father in-law for his unasked for interference.

As I was on the point of departing, I came upon a colleague in the ante-room of the manager, whom I had already met very often, and who, as I knew, was likewise waiting for an appointment, only, unlike me, not during two, but four years. I told him that I had just obtained an appointment, and described it on being questioned more minutely. He thereupon changed color suddenly, and would have sunk to the ground, if I had not quickly caught him. Full of painful anticipations, I demanded the reason of this striking behavior, and then learnt that the appointment which had been given to me was the one for which he had been hoping for a long time. Now I knew that the unfortunate man had already been employed by the establishment once before, had given perfect satisfaction in the performance of his duties, and had only been dismissed because the department in which he had been employed had been dissolved. Besides this, he was married, was father of four children, and had by degrees fallen into the deepest misery during the long time that he had had to wait. His last possession was already pledged, and his family was irremediably in danger of dying from starvation. He told me all this, gulping forth the words with difficulty, and his eyes sparkled very uneasily as if from the thought of a razor, charcoal vapor, or other means of suicide.

My determination was immediately taken. I asked the poor man to wait for me, and called on the manager again. I told him what I had learnt in short dry words, gave my deed of appointment back to him again, and asked him to procure the appointment for the older and better entitled candidate.

"If you will not have it," he said, "there are aspirants in abundance who will come before your *protégé*. I pity the poor wretch, but what must I do? No less than seven candidates for this place are under the patronage of various influential persons, and it has not been hitherto given away because these various influences keep the balance equally poised. Your connexions are decidedly better than those of all the others, and this has put an end to the balancing. Do you look at me contemptuously and indignantly? Do you suppose that protected children are dearer to me than deserving colleagues? Am I then master here? Do not I myself depend upon those influences which give appointments in this manner? If I took it into my head to fight against patronage, they would very soon sweep me away. Believe me, my young friend, one must howl with the wolves, and he who does not like being hammer, will soon find himself become an anvil upon which others will hammer with all their might. If you do not see that, you are not fit for our business, and I can only advise you to turn your back on us as soon as possible."

I told the prudent man of business, whom I could not accuse of being unjust in other matters, that he might do what he could and would with the appointment; I, for my part, resigned it altogether. I told my fellow candidate outside what had happened, and handed him a sum sufficiently large to keep him and his family from want for a long time, but on the way advised him to pack up and emigrate to Freeland.

Half an hour later I had an explanation with the father of the lady to whom I was engaged. I wanted to reproach him for his unasked interference, but he had scarcely learned what had happened when he turned the tables and loaded me with the most violent reproaches. He said that I was insane and quite unfit for the seriousness of life, that he had already repented for some time past of having given his consent to his daughter marrying such a silly person, and that now his patience was at an end. I might go to the devil and practice my philanthropical ideas elsewhere.

The angel whom I wished to make my own witnessed this scene. For a moment I hoped to see her whom my heart had chosen take my own part. She did not do so; on the contrary she took her father's side, and only shyly attempted to plead alleviating circumstances in my favor; I am still young, she said, a moment of effervescence of feeling has overcome me, she could not give up the hope that when I have become prudent through misfortune, I would renounce these follies for the future. But when I declared that I had acted after ripe forethought, and when I added to this that I must despise myself if I could ever act otherwise, she turned her back on me contemptuously.

When she saw that I prepared to depart without making reparation, she made yet another attempt to hold me fast with tears and supplication. But the gist of all her entreaties was always again and again, I may yet become a reasonable man and cease to vex myself about the concerns of strangers. The charm which until then had bound me to the graceful creature was altogether destroyed. I perceived that I had been worshiping an unfeeling doll. What

I had at first regarded as a sacrifice to the truth of my convictions—the rupture with her—that took, the more she spoke and wept, the form of a reward. I saw that my way of acting had prevented me from being sacrificed to a mistake which I had made in choosing my future wife. The object of my tenderness at last perceived that herself, and I took my departure amidst angry words.

Thus was the last bond which held me fast broken. My affairs here were arranged in a few days, and then I set out for Freeland.

CHAPTER II.

THE JOURNEY.

I CHOSE a Freeland ship for the journey to the "Land of Liberty." Certain misgivings had indeed occurred to me through the fact that there is no class distinction on the large steamships which this state has been running for some years between the coast of East Africa and the chief parts of Europe and America. For since those ships as a rule take more than a thousand emigrants, I entertained some doubt with regard to the convenience of places where equality prevailed, and I was for a moment tempted to make the sea voyage in a French ship or in one of the English P. & O. steamers. Meanwhile the wish to be acquainted with the inhabitants of Freeland as soon as possible decided me, and so I went to the nearest agency for Freeland, and booked a passage on the "Urania," which was to leave Trieste on the second of May.

I was not sorry for this choice. There were no fewer than eleven hundred and sixty passengers, but the ships which belong to Freeland are so arranged that every party finds separate accommodation in clean, convenient, and partitioned off cabins. During the day the passengers live in large and agreeable dining and drawing rooms. At night every individual who is traveling by himself, and every family, has a private sleeping apartment. Since the heat was very great, especially during the passage through the Red Sea, fresh air was pumped through every part of the ship by a powerful ventilating apparatus, and everything was kept sufficiently cool. The catering, too, was excellent, and the cleanliness above all praise.

I will not mention any of the events of the voyage. We passed the Suez Canal on the eighth of May, and on the nineteenth of the same month we anchored in the roads of Lamu. This place was an inconsiderable haunt of Arabs only seven years ago, when Freeland was founded; it is now a great commercial town endowed with all the appliances of modern commerce. The English, to whom the place belongs, have understood how to make the best use of the advantages which Freeland has granted to them.

The immigration to Freeland, which, with diminishing exceptions, takes the direction over Lamu and the mouth of the Tana reached the number of 500,000 souls last year, and is steadily increasing. The value of the goods exported during the seven years amounted to ninety-two million pounds sterling, and goods to this value were also imported. The business is entirely in the hands of the commonwealth of Freeland, but the English and all the people who live on the coast as a matter of course get enormous advantages from it, as is clearly shown by the rapid increase of Lamu, and the evident prosperity of the people who live there.

I went on shore, together with the greater part of my fellow passengers, at Lamu, where great hotels which belonged to Freeland received us. Only a small part, not quite two hundred, immediately went on board a small steamboat which was lying in the roads. This vessel sailed round the promontory of Rasshaga, and ran through the bay of Ungana straight into the mouth of the Tana. This direct entrance into the river, which also served us later on as a way into our new home, is sometimes dangerous if the wind does not blow in the right direction, for the Tana has a bar heaped up at its mouth, which is, as formerly, almost quite impassable, and even now, after it has been dredged, ships meet with difficult obstacles. The breakers have to be passed, and these wash over the deck in a disagreeable manner. This necessarily causes one to be hurled hither and thither, but that does not do much harm, especially to those who have just successfully performed a seventeen days' sea voyage.

The greater number of the passengers, and I was among them, preferred, as I have said, to avoid the bar of the Tana by an overland passage. Lamu is situated on an island which is separated from the mainland by a narrow channel, and lies opposite to a bay which extends far into the land. The English have made a railway to the lower Tana from the extreme point of the bay where the Mkonambi district lies. This railway we then proceeded to use.

At Engatana, where we reached the Tana, river boats belonging to Freeland received us. Five steamboats to which signals had been made were ready to convey the nine hundred passengers. The Tana is a very large river, as broad and deep as the Rhine at Cologne or the Danube at Vienna, and I could not therefore conceive why larger ships were not built. I solved the problem later on when we reached Odaboruruwa after a fourteen hours' passage. Above that place the Tana is divided into numerous branches which are so intricately intertwined that larger, and especially longer, ships would easily get grounded. On that account the government of Freeland prefers to let smaller vessels ply, which therefore have the advantage of being able to take passengers, without having to turn back, to Hargazo, where the rapids and cataracts begin, and the river is quite unnavigable.

I will briefly pass over the twenty hours' voyage on the Tana from Engatana to Hargazo. It was fairly uniform till we got to Odaboruruwa. The shores of this magnificent river are bordered on both sides by thickets and forests which render the back ground quite invisible. The forests along these shores are frequently interrupted by luxuriant settlements of the black aborigines or of the white immigrants, and their settlements are so very much like one another with their clean little houses shaded by banana trees, and with their luxurious fields and fruit groves, that after a few hours they no longer attract attention. The scenery of Odaboruruwa is quite different. Here the numerous islands and windings of the river always offer new and ravishing prospects, and the river, which contains a great quantity of fish right down to the mouth, begins to show an extremely lively animal world. Flamingoes in myriads occupied all the shallow places along the shore. Hippopotami are so numerous and closely packed together in some places, that it almost appeared as if they would stop the passage of the ships. But the uncouth fellows always vanished by diving with incredible agility before the steamboat reached them, but only to reappear again some distance off. Not so quick, however, are the crocodiles which likewise lie in great numbers on all the sunny parts of the shore, and trusting to their coats of mail, allow the steamboats to approach in a very unconcerned manner.

We reached Hargazo towards midnight. This is the place where the passengers change from the boat passage of the Tana to the Freeland railway. Here the inhabitants of Freeland have founded their first settlement, which, however, still lies without their own district. It is designed to afford shelter to travelers, and a noble land and garden husbandry serves for the purpose of producing on the spot what is necessary for the numerous and daily changing strangers. The fruitfulness of the land is here extraordinary and surpassing all description. The rapidity of the river which commences above the place enables the rich marsh land to be well irrigated, and the hot equatorial sun, for Hargazo lies only half a degree south of the equator, ripens every kind of fruit to perfection in a fabulously short space of time. For this reason a hundred and twenty and hundred and fifty fold harvest of corn twice a year is the rule here.

I only stopped at Hargazo for a day, and I must say that in spite of its equatorial position, and the fact that it is not quite three hundred meters above the level of the sea, I felt the heat very little. The country already begins to be mountainous here. Cool and shady valleys run straight up to the river, and, as there is no marsh in the neighborhood, I think that the place is perfectly healthy. But in spite of this, the Freeland colonists do not look upon Hargazo as a permanent place of settlement. The inhabitants only remain here for a short time, and at the latest are relieved at the end of a year by others. The inhabitants of Freeland have noticed that the continued, if not excessive heat, which is felt everywhere in the equatorial lowlands, cannot be endured for long by Europeans. Some months or even a year of it can be endured without difficulty, but loss of appetite is soon added to other burdensome liver complaints. As the inhabitants are not obliged to endanger their health to find a livelihood, they avoid exposing a year of their lives unnecessarily to such dangers.

After a day's stoppage, I steamed north-westwards to Kenia on the railway. The expression "steamed" must only be understood in a figurative sense here, for the lines in this country are not worked by steam, but by electricity. The rapids and cataracts of the Tana furnish the electric power necessary for this purpose, and for a number of other commercial and industrial undertakings. To understand this, one must know that the river from Hargazo to Kikuyu makes a chain of rapids and waterfalls, the grandeur of which has no equal in the world. The Tana has a fall of five thousand feet along this course, and some of the cataracts have a fall of three hundred feet. There is here a motive force of many millions of horse power to be disposed of, and in spite of the fact that the community has hitherto tapped this source of power in an extravagant manner for the two and a half millions which its population numbered at that time, there is always enough at hand for other purposes.

The Tana also provided further for our advancement after we had left it. The force of gravitation which had already accumulated in its waters during their passage from Kenia to the valley being now changed into electricity serves to lift us up to Kenia through all the windings of the mighty chain of mountains which we now entered.

Our passage over the two hundred and eighty chiliometers of the railway from the Tana to Kenia occupied twelve hours. At the end of next year, when the new railway from the Tana to Kenia, which has been already commenced, is finished, the journey will only take four hours. The line which was in use at that time was a temporary structure which the community had taken in hand and completed in the second year of its existence. It has a number of sharp curves and steep ascents, and the bridges and viaducts are all made of wood. All this tends to make traveling slow.

The romantic grandeur of the mountainous region into which we entered soon after leaving Hargazo surpasses all description. The giant mountains at whose feet and sides the railway began to ascend are twelve thousand feet high. Their slopes are covered partly by majestic and very old forests, partly by park-like meadows, and the remainder looks wild and gloomy. We had our mid-day rest in a valley whose smiling sweetness reminded us of the Italian Alps. An hour later the train rolled through a wilderness of rough rocks of awful desolation in which there was not a single blade of grass, and no wild animal interrupted the death-like stillness. Again, an hour later, we passed through a broad valley which appeared to be filled by numerous herds of placidly browsing antelopes, zebras, buffaloes, rhinoceroses, and elephants.

But all that we had hitherto seen was greatly eclipsed when, at about four o'clock in the afternoon, the train had climbed the ridge of the bulwark of mountains which separates Kenia from the Tana, and the glacier region of Kenia presented itself to our ravished gaze. The sultriness which had until then been tolerably overpowering was changed into a refreshing coolness caused by the breezes which blew down from Kenia. We had reached the high table-lands of Freeland, and entered into Washington, the first railway station in Freeland, at about five o'clock in the afternoon.

I will not stop to describe this place. At eight o'clock in the evening we arrived at Edendale, the capital of Freeland. The station-yard and all the streets which I passed through on the way to the hotel were lighted up as bright as day by arc electric lamps. I hardly saw any house at all on this occasion of my first passing through Edendale, for the streets are all bordered by several rows of palm trees, and the houses themselves lie all together in the midst of luxurious gardens, so that all one could see of them was the glittering of lighted up windows. But my ears told me all the more that Edendale was no city of the dead. Music, the clattering of cups, and jovial laughter sounded in numerous gardens which I passed by. But I was too tired and wearied by the journey to feel any temptation to take part in the common gaiety. The omnibus which I and seven of my traveling companions had entered at the station-yard set us down after a quarter of an hour's ride at one of the great hotels which are kept by companies in this country.

When I had partaken of a simple meal I went to bed, and in spite of the feverish expectation with which I looked forward to the next day, I soon fell into a deep and refreshing sleep.

CHAPTER III.

WHERE FREELAND IS SITUATED AND WHAT IT IS.

NOW the reader has been good enough to follow me to the capital of Freeland, it is time to tell him more minutely where the town and country are situated, what conditions obtain, and what I in particular seek here. I have hitherto supposed that he knows all that as well as I do; and in fact both Freeland and the justice in economic matters which exists there have been much talked about for seven years. But if I see that all this is already known, I write for those who either do not know at all, or are only slightly aware of it, so that the stage upon which events which are narrated in the following chapters take place may be described and we can proceed with our story.

Freeland is a social free state which was founded seven years ago on the Kenia highlands by a couple of thousand enthusiasts. If one follows the east coast of Africa on the map from Cape Guardafui southwards to the Equator, and if one then goes by an imaginary line toward the west into the interior of the continent, he will find Kenia not quite five hundred chiliometers from the coast of the Indian Ocean. It is a mountain which would be reckoned as the grandest and most remarkable on the whole globe, even if the inhabitants of Freeland had not happened to settle at its foot. It is no single peak, but a huge mass of mountains, the central peak of which is nearly six thousand meters high and projects into the regions of ice and snow. But the peculiarity of Kenia, is that it, unlike the Kilima Ndsharo mountains, which lie five hundred chiliometers to the south and resemble it in the magnitude of other details, does not rise directly from the lower plain, but has a plateau which is from twelve hundred to two thousand two hundred meters above the level of the sea and several hundreds of chiliometers wide, surrounding it on all sides. And this table-land, which is broken up by several more or less huge and highly picturesque chains of mountains and watered by many rivers, streams and lakes, some of which rise in Kenia itself, and some in the gigantic mountains in front, builds up the territory of Freeland.

So much for the geography of my present home. In the meantime I will only say this much about its political and social constitution, that it has realized what has been the ideal of mankind for two-and-a-half centuries, namely: perfect equality of rights with regard to economic life. The people of Freeland are not· communists. They do not go upon the assumption that all men are simply equal, but they acknowledge their differences with regard to ability and wants. What they think is that all men have equal rights, and by equal rights they do not merely mean that all men possess equally the recognized privilege of choosing representatives, paying taxes, being imprisoned, and allowing themselves to be shot for their country, but also that all men possess the right to live. They maintain that all other freely accorded liberties are not in the least useful to the man who has to depend upon the good will of another for being able to use his own powers for continuing his life, but that he is rather the servant of that man upon whose good will his existence depends.

But the people of Freeland have not contented themselves with announcing this right, which a man has to his life, as a principle; they have gone further and have guaranteed to every man those means which are necessary to make a practical use of this important inborn right. They do not think that everyone should be provided directly with that which he needs for keeping himself alive, or that the community should interfere with single individuals. They are rather of the opinion that it should be everyone's business to take care of himself. "To everyone his own" is their motto, which is quite similar to that of the rest of the world, but with the difference that everyone may own what is his property according to the constitution of Freeland, that is, what he produces himself, whilst according to the constitution of the outside world, a man may own anything whatever, as long as he has not thereby offended against the laws of murder, robbery, theft, and fraud.

Furthermore the Freelanders do not believe that any artificial organization is necessary to regulate human labor on these principles. They have thus nothing in common with the earlier Socialists or Communists on this important point. They rather adhere to the maxim of the rest of the world that the greatest possible harmony of all economic interests comes of itself through the free play of economical forces. They say that there is nothing else necessary to ensure that all the needs of the community should be provided for in the best imaginable way than to let every single person act as much as possible without disturbance under the incitement of his natural inborn motives for labor. The opinion that it is necessary that the state should interfere in some manner, for those things to be produced of which man has the greatest need, comes to the same thing as if it were thought to be necessary to keep the water of a river in vats and barrels at the bottom of a valley from fear that otherwise it would flow up the mountain. Where everything that a man produces belongs to him, and where there is a free market at which his products can be exchanged for goods which he needs, it is then quite plain that everyone will produce what is needed by the community, because only under this supposition can he fulfil the purpose of his industry, which consists in nothing else than in the desire to supply his own needs as perfectly as possible with the least possible trouble. But everyone can do that only if he manufactures such things as correspond to his needs. Therefore giving perfect freedom to the selfishness of the workman is the best method of organizing the production in a manner corresponding to the benefit of the community.

The reader will see at once that this is exactly the doctrine which Adam Smith put forth a century and a half ago. Its correctness does not require to be proved.' Only those few have hitherto given up the opinion that this operation of free acting self-interest leads to the highest economic harmony, who go on the supposition that not all, but only some men can and will do what their own interests teach them. They think that the great majority must be compelled to make not what they need themselves, but what others need, and then only that that will happen which is necessary for all. The doctrine of Adam Smith is accepted literally in Freeland. The obstacles which oppose the operations of self-interest are all cleared away, and the people are quite convinced that the result will be in correspondence with the interests of all. The inhabitants of Freeland think that using artificial measures and contrivances of any kind to make work thrive are always altogether superfluous. They maintain that the economical and social laws current among them are quite suitable for human nature, and that a perfectly natural condition of things arises and is developed spontaneously. Liberalism, as is well known, says the same thing, and it declares that the economical and social condition, as it would have it, corresponds with human nature. And it also deduces from this the conclusion that labor would thrive and develope in the best possible manner if left to itself without interference. It is as clear as daylight, at least to me, upon which side the truth lies. I believe that it is not in human nature to work so that others should enjoy what one has produced, and that the economy of the rest of the world could not be maintained for one day if it was handed over to its own resources, that is, if the protection of the state was withdrawn from it. In order to make prevailing social laws suitable to the world in general, nine tenths of mankind would have to be compelled to obey them, for these laws are contrary to their oldest and most important interests. The economy of Freeland did not, on the contrary, need such a defense for its continual stability because all interests are equally guarded in it. In order to disturb social order here, single individuals must possess the power to impose their will upon others. But, in consequence of the previously restored equality of rights, they do not possess this power, and as long as this is the case, it cannot happen that any inhabitants of Freeland is dependent on the good will and caprice of a fellow creature. It can and often does happen in Freeland that some particular person, because he is more skilful, industrious, or frugal than another, becomes richer than he does, but these greater riches he can only use to enjoy himself more than others, and not for the purpose of making them serve him. For the most unskilful, most negligent, and most careless inhabitant of Freeland is not dependent on the wealth of another when he does any work, since everything which he needs for his help, both land and capital, can always be had to be employed as he pleases.

These are the outlines of the organization which exists in Freeland. One sees that in its essence it aims at nothing else but the realization of those principles which the rest of the world has always claimed as its own but never followed. Freeland is the final verification of all that which the civilized world has hitherto set before itself. It does nothing else than what modern Liberalism claims to have always done. It proclaims equality of rights, as the rest of the world also does, but it makes equality of rights a truth, and the rest of the world makes it a lie. What the latter realizes is exploitation.

Freeland promulgates Liberty; the rest of the world does likewise. But the Liberty of Freeland is a verity; that of the *bourgeois* world is false, its true name being Slavery. It proclaims self-interest to be the inducement to work, but in Freeland only is labor expended for the laborer's own advantage, whilst the rest of the world only pretends that self-interest furnishes the incitement to work. What it recognizes as work is done for the advantage of others, or advantage from the work of another.

The way in which all these principles find their practical accomplishment in Freeland is explained in what follows. But it can do no harm if I give the fundamental laws of Freeland *in extenso* as a preliminary. They consist only of five clauses, which are :—

(1) Every inhabitant of Freeland has an equal inalienable

right to the common land and to the means of production which are furnished by the state.

(2) Women, children, and old men, and those who are unfit for work have a right to sufficient maintenance corresponding to the amount of wealth belonging to the state.

(3) No one can be hindered in executing his own free individual will as long as he does not interfere with the rights of others.

(4) Matters of public interest are decided by all he inhabitants of Freeland who are of the requisite age (over twenty-five years) without distinction of sex. All these possess the same active and passive rights of speaking and voting in everything that concerns the state.

(5) The legislative and executive powers are divided according to the branches of business in such a manner that the totality of those who have the right of voting choose separate representatives for each of the principal branches of public business. These form their decisions apart, and watch over the working of the organs of administration which belong to each.

CHAPTER IV.

WHO CLEANED MY BOOTS IN FREELAND, THE APPEARANCE OF THE STREETS, AND THE OWNERSHIP OF DWELLING HOUSES.

THE sun was already high in the heavens when I awoke on the first morning of my stay at Edendale. In spite of this it was still quite cold, and the balmy air blew into the open window in quite a refreshing manner, so that I was glad of the pleasing warmth of the bedclothes which I had heaped up heavily and thickly the night before. Edendale lies just on the Equator and I should not much wonder if that mathematical line goes just through my room. One would thus suppose that it is always uniformly hot here, and that special precautions against the cold of the night are quite unnecessary. But that is not so, for a maximum and minimum thermometer placed close to my bed showed that the temperature had fallen to nine degrees centigrade during the night, and even now, although it was eight o'clock in the morning, it had only just reached fifteen degrees centigrade.

I had slept for two hours after sunrise, which in these latitudes always takes place at six o'clock. This vexed me, for I was impatient to know more about the town and the manner in which things are done in Freeland. I therefore determined to get up at once.

The button of an electric bell which was visible at the head of my bed informed me, to my astonishment, that here one can be served when one wishes. A man entered the room a few seconds after I had rung. As regards clothing and other details, he was not at all different from the other inhabitants of Freeland whom I had noticed during the journey. He asked me what I wished for in a polite, but firm business-like voice.

"Excuse my troubling you," I said as I opened the conversation, "I know very well that everyone is equal in Freeland and that there are no masters or servants. But this bell tempted me to use it, and so I beg you to tell me as a stranger firstly, why there are bells in the bedrooms of the hotels in Freeland, and secondly, where I can get the things requisite for cleaning my clothes?"

"Your conjecture about the bell has not deceived you," was his laughing reply. "I am one of the six hotel servants who are here alternately night and day to attend to our guests. I venture to tell you that for the future you can not do better than hang up your clothes on the hook which is fixed into your door for this purpose when you want them cleaned. For every time you ring, it costs exactly half as much as the use of a room for a whole day, that is, two-and-a-half pence. But if you act in the way that I have explained, your clothes and boots will be put in the same place in the morning when they have been brought back from the cleaners. This also costs two-and-a-half pence, and you spare me needless exercise."

"So you are a kind of footman," I could not help asking, "and there are domestic servants for cleaning clothes and boots here? How does this agree with the equality which exists in Freeland, and why does sending for you once cost as much as the day's work of a domestic servant, and both together as much as the hire of this neatly arranged room for a day?"

"Equality," he replied, "as we understand the word in Freeland is not in the least infringed because I and my colleagues of 'the Association for rendering Personal Services' are at your beck and call, and other colleagues of the same society clean your clothes. We are really business men and workmen who make our living by doing this. Would your personal dignity be injured if you were to clean boots or clothes for us to-morrow, or build houses, or write books. Everyone performs what he can and what corresponds best to his own needs, and we only recognize a difference in so far as disagreeable duties or those which demand a greater amount of special ability must be better compensated than those which are lighter and more agreeable and only demand ordinary ability. I could, for example, make my living quite as well as gardener or as clerk in any office, but as a gardener I would only earn three and a half shillings an hour because that kind of work is both light and agreeable. The sedentary mode of life in an office does not please me, and so I have chosen the business in which I am now engaged and at which I make nearly five shillings an hour. In the performance of my duties I can take sufficient exercise, which is very valuable to me, and besides I can make very interesting acquaintances, which is very much in accordance with my disposition. Besides, I consider myself a gentleman, and all my fellow citizens think the same about me. If I only had the necessary means, nobody in Freeland would hesitate to give me his support as a candidate for the administration if I asked for it. The case is exactly the same with my colleagues who clean clothes; nobody ever thinks of making any distinction between their work and that of any other person. What should we come to if that happened? One cannot be compelled to do any work here. Everyone of us is free to choose his profession as long as he is fitted for it. Should the least stain be attached in public opinion to any one of these kinds of employment, nobody would be found to perform them. Then you would be compelled to clean your clothes yourself, to arrange your room yourself, and so on, while you are perhaps a scholar whose time is far more profitably employed with other thoughts, or a man of business who employs his time more usefully in a different occupation."

"But, as concerns the price of our services, that is arranged, as the price of all other things is in Freeland, according to the necessary expense of the work. It is true that the discharge of a small commission, which you lay upon me, seemingly costs as little time as the detailed and careful cleaning of your clothes. But that is only apparently so. I and my colleagues have to always be ready to comply with any chance wish of yours, even during the night, as it is always possible that for some reason or other, as for example a sudden illness, you may be in want of us. For that reason six attendants, who are on duty day and night alternately, are appointed to this hotel, and you will be of the opinion that it is only just that we should have some compensation for the time spent in waiting. The process of cleaning the clothes can, on the contrary, be accomplished at one time for all the guests in the hotel, and as very ingenious machines are employed for this purpose, the amount of time consumed by the workmen engaged in this employment is very small in proportion. And the rent of the rooms is nothing else than the sum of money which is required to pay the expenses of the room during all the time that it is usable. Five pennies a day makes one hundred and fifty shillings per annum, if one reckoned that there are three hundred days in the year during which the room is let. This is quite enough to pay off the capital spent on it till the time that it ceases to be used, and to cover necessary repairs and refitting."

I must confess that the certainty of not having to clean my boots myself in Freeland removed a weight from my heart in spite of all my enthusiasm for the equality of rights. Indeed I had not been obliged to perform this operation during the whole journey on the steamboat as well as at Lamu and Hargazo, but I had explained this to myself by supposing that the inhabitants of Freeland when outside their own country are not entirely under the control of their own administration. This opinion was especially strengthened by the fact that there were negroes in Lamu and Hargazo whom I found occupied in serving the travelers. But I had imagined that these negroes were employed by the Freelanders as menials and for occupations which they would not undertake themselves. This now appeared to be a mistake, and I will remark that the black servants in Lamu and Hargazo are also united into an association and are organized upon exactly the same principles as their Caucasian fellow workmen in Freeland.

When I had dressed myself, I had my breakfast in the dining room of the hotel. This is not supplied by the hotel company, but by the Edendale Food Company, for the hotel company only attends to the building and its organization and confines itself in other respects to superintending the whole management. Then I went out into the streets.

It was nearly ten o'clock now, and tolerably warm, the thermometer indicating 22 degrees centigrade in the shade. I will observe here that the heat is, as a rule, greatest at eleven o'clock, and that on this first day, which was towards the end of May, the hottest month in the year, the temperature went up to 28 degrees centigrade. The greatest heat which occurs here during the year is 32 degrees centigrade, a very tolerable warmth which is only seldom reached, and is in no wise as frequent as it is in Europe with the exception of only England, Norway, and Northern Russia. Here, however, on the equator, at a height of 1700 meters above the level of the sea, one knows nothing of that torment of men and animals which what is known as a hot summer's day usually brings with it in temperate Europe. And this for various reasons. Firstly the air is so pure and clear that the feeling of anxious oppression which great heat generally causes in our latitudes cannot occur. Secondly, refreshing breezes blow down from Kenia at the hottest hours of the day. Thirdly, and this is the principal cause of the moderate temperature, one is well acquainted here with all the means of keeping off the heat of the sun. No one works in the open air during the middle part of the day, and at this time only a few operations are kept going in cool and pleasantly covered workshops. The inhabitants of Freeland eat, bathe, rest, and read from twelve o'clock to three o'clock in the afternoon. The streets are also less thronged during this time in spite of the fact that thick rows of palm trees, which grow everywhere, prevent the heat from getting troublesome with their deep cool shadows.

These beautiful groves and the wonderful gardens which surround them on all sides give a characteristic stamp to Edendale. Every family in Freeland dwells in its own house, and every house is surrounded by its great garden a thousand square meters in extent. These houses are the private property of the inhabitants and serve, like the gardens, for their private use. The inhabitants of Freeland do not, as a rule, recognize any kind of ownership of land; they rather go upon the principle that the land must be put into everyone's hand to do what he chooses with. This, in the most literal and wide sense of the word, means that every inhabitant of Freeland can cultivate every piece of land whenever he pleases. But this only relates to the land which is set apart for cultivation, and not to that set apart for living upon. It does not follow that because, according to the constitution of Freeland, everyone may employ his working power where he pleases, he cannot claim the right to a piece of earth as his own where he can set up a dwelling undisturbed by everyone else. Even animals have their holes and nests quite to themselves, and share them with no one else, but in spite of this, they do not recognize the ownership of land. The difference between the primordial natural right and the right which exists in Freeland with regard to this, only consists in the fact that animals choose their places of abode capriciously and accidentally, whereas the inhabitants of Freeland have agreed, with regard to the size and disposition of the land serving for the creation of a dwelling house, to form regulations, and a kind of building court, which has jurisdiction in such matters. This court has to determine what ground is and what is not to be built upon, it parcels out the land for building, sees to the laying out of streets, canals, and the like, and especially takes care that not more than one building is erected upon one building allotment. Nobody is forbidden to erect his dwelling house on land that is lying fallow without the express permission of the building court, but he has himself to blame, if later on other people happen to wish to use the ground for other purposes, and he has neither the right nor power to hinder them from doing this, but must do the best he can, according to the circumstances. To prevent this from happening, and to get complete compensation in case the ground chosen as a site for a dwelling house may perhaps be afterwards claimed for other purposes, the consent of the building court, which in this case represents the state, must be obtained. One must therefore either use for building those allotments which have been previously assigned by the building court for that purpose, or one must obtain the approbation of the court if one wishes to build anywhere else. No tax for the use of the site is imposed.

The reader will now notice that the exclusive right of use is only valid on the supposition that the building site is used for the erection of one's own building. Nobody would be prevented from making a business of building and letting houses if he wished to do so. But, if other people wish to use the ground thus built upon, it again becomes public property, and, indeed, unless he obtained the assent of the building court that the land should be used for such purposes, he has not even any title to compensation for the buildings erected. There are naturally no hired houses in Freeland which are owned by private persons. There are of course companies, whose business is the letting of dwelling places, but as the right of joining these or any of the other companies in Freeland is always open to every-one, exactly the same rule applies to the land built upon by them as to all other land in Freeland; everyone who wishes can make use of it.

I shall continue this subject later on. I will only remark here that it does not occur to any inhabitant of Freeland to build his house himself, after the manner of the backwoodsmen in North America. He lets the building companies do this for him and pays for their work, either all at once, or in annual instalments, according to their wishes, which last, it may be noticed in passing, are in this case not paid to the building companies, but to the State, as all companies in Freeland have had their funds advanced by the state. The houses which have been acquired by purchase naturally belong to the purchaser absolutely. He can sell, give away, exchange, or transfer them just as he pleases.

The inhabitants of Edendale have houses corresponding to the means of their owners and very different in size and equipment. There are some which have no more than five habitable rooms, and some which have as many as twenty. Some are very simple, others are furnished with taste and luxury. One can read their age with tolerable exactness on their exterior; the oldest date from the first two years after Freeland had been founded and are wooden barracks. I was told that there are a very few of these in existence now, only six in the whole of Edendale, whilst all other buildings of that epoch have long since been replaced by newer, finer, and more comfortable ones, for the wealth of the inhabitants of Freeland has been very rapidly increasing, and at this time the most simple laborers possessed an income sufficiently great to allow the luxury of a fine and pleasant house. They have been building in bricks, stone, and iron since five years, and the execution becomes richer and more perfect from year to year. I shall have to describe what the houses are like inside later on.

There is a great number of public buildings in Edendale. The most prominent are the Public and Administrative Palace, the Central Bank, the University, the Academy of Arts, three Public Libraries, four Theaters, the Grand Central Goods Warehouse,—a building covering a space of four hecatares, a great number of Schools, and many other buildings. What strikes one with most of these public buildings is the extraordinary splendor with which they are decorated, and it is clear that the inhabitants of Freeland have great talent for the fine arts, and employ this in a very high degree in their public edifices. They resemble in this respect the ancient Athenæans, whose household arrangements were very modest, whilst no expense was thought to be too great for the fine embellishment of their public buildings. I learned later on that the administration of Freeland not only employs a great number of artists, who work at the decoration, but also buys every work of art that is offered to it and which the critics think sufficiently good for the decoration of any public building or place. The reader will be able for the first time to estimate what flights high art must take under such circumstances when I come to speak of the immense resources which are in the power of the administration of Freeland.

Very extraordinary means are taken to provide for the public health and cleanliness. The aqueducts of Edendale are to-day almost without any equal in the world, and they are being extended daily. The refuse is cleared away by a system of pneumatic sucking apparatus. The streets are entirely macadamized, and no trace of dust or dirt is visible upon them. They are crossed in all directions by a net-work of electric tramways which connect all the suburbs with the town. The factories are placed altogether in the suburbs, so that the idyllic rest of the town, which is only interrupted by the songs of the birds and the laughing of children, is not disturbed anywhere by disagreeable noises. The trotting of horses is not heard anywhere. Carriages are used, but they are not drawn by horses, but by mechanical power, electricity being principally used for this purpose. There is no scarcity of horses in Edendale ; on the contrary the inhabitants are passionately fond of riding, but the horses are only used for excursions outside the precincts of the town, and the stables are not situated near the private houses, but are in the hands of the great transport companies, whose stable men and attendants do not carry on their work in the way that we do it, but they conduct it, as is almost always the case in Freeland, almost completely with the aid of machines, so that on the average one workman can attend to fifty horses. Keeping these animals is a luxury which every laborer in Freeland can enjoy if he pleases, in spite of the fact that the "stable servants" ask for and get the average pay that every other workman in Freeland has.

CHAPTER V.

HOW I CHOSE A BUSINESS IN FREELAND, AND PAID FOR MY DINNER AT THE RESTAURANT.

WHEN I had spent some hours in satisfying my curiosity by inspecting what was most worth seeing in Edendale, in which operation the inhabitants of Freeland whom I happened to meet willingly acted as guides and explained everything, I determined to make preliminary inquiries as to what steps I ought to take concerning my future occupation in Freeland. I knew that all the work here, as far as it is not, like the post, telegraph, railways, etc., under the control of the state, is in the hands of great manufacturing companies which divide their profits among their members, that everyone has the right of belonging to one of these companies, and that it was only necessary to choose one which suited my abilities and tastes. I also knew that every care is taken to give help to the public so that they can select the right business. They had advised me to go first of all, for the sake of convenience, to the intelligence department of the Central Statistical Office, and so I directed my steps thither.

The functionary who received me asked to which branch of occupation I thought of directing my attention. My particular speciality was hitherto machinery in its application to the working of railways. I learnt that the pay of engineers in this branch was not as much as it is in other workshops. "But that must not prevent you," he added, "from turning your attention to this branch if you believe that you are specially suitable for it, because in this case you can reckon to make up for the small pay which you will have at starting by rapid promotion."

"I cannot very well rely on this," I replied, being unconsciously affected by my European experience. "Who knows if I would certainly succeed in getting compensation corresponding to my abilities?"

"You appear to forget," he replied laughing, "that there is in Freeland a company suitable for all the pursuits into which you wish to enter. In order that your abilities should not get their proper reward here, you must intentionally hide them. It is quite impossible here that eminent abilities should remain unnoticed. Whether you get a post which is suitable for you will depend on your superiors, but they are so far dependent upon those who are placed under their authority that they are indebted for their position to a choice which is always revocable, and you can see that this revocation would certainly take place if the managers let themselves be guided in their decisions by any other than purely business motives."

"And who," I asked, "ensures that these subordinates interest themselves in me in case I am unjustly treated?"

"Their own interest does this. They are not hirelings with fixed pay, but they have a right to equal shares, and the amount of the share which they get from the undertaking always depends upon the greater or less fitness or skill with which the business is managed. Can you not imagine that anywhere in Europe where the owner of a business is also the manager, you would be placed in the right position if he knew where you would be most profitable to him. In Freeland, your colleagues will be the masters of whatever business you enter into."

The reader can understand that these explanations gave me great tranquillity. I further enquired, if only for the sake of information, whether there was any security that my future superiors would not enter into some agreement with my future colleagues, and would perhaps even use artifice by their express commands in order to make any participation in their business disagreeable to me.

"To make that possible," said my informer, "such a

command would not only have to be secretly made, but also secretly executed, so that no one should know that a desire for seclusion prevailed in the company in question. For our fundamental law lays down that everyone shall have perfect freedom to enter into any company which may be suitable for him. The manager or whoever else the general assembly entrusts with this duty of course has the right of deciding in what manner the candidate shall be employed. They can leave unemployed those who, in their judgment, are quite unsuitable, or use them for mere handwork. Everyone gets his share out of the business only according to the amount of effective work which he does, and if he did not succeed in performing any service, he would get little or nothing from his abilities. As soon as public opinion came to the conclusion that suitable workmen were wilfully kept away, the intrigue would be at an end."

"Why so?" I asked. "The companies have no connexion whatever with one another, the state does not interfere, and, if I am rightly informed, it rests in the hands of the members to decide upon everything which concerns th business."

"You are rightly informed in this respect, but you forget that every inhabitant of Freeland has the right to become a member of any business that he pleases. One only has to present oneself for this purpose, for the managers only decide upon the manner in which the members are to be employed, and not on the membership itself. You will now perceive that no one in Freeland could look on without feeling anxious if any company transgressed against the right of working men to enter into any kind of employment that they please, which is the foundation of our social organization. Everyone must always be permitted to have that kind of employment which is most in accordance with his abilities, and all the country knows that the conscientious observance of this principle is the supposition upon which our liberty and prosperity are built up. Should it be noticed that this principle is violated anywhere, half of the working people of Freeland would present themselves to such a company, merely for the purpose of settling the management through their vote in the general assembly. All that is so easily understood that fools would be the only people to make such experiments, and there is hardly any manager who would be disposed to act in such a way."

"I am quite satisfied on this point," I answered, "but you must allow me to state the objections to this. Since it is so dangerous to dismiss fit workmen, and opinions concerning fitness and completeness vary considerably, I think that our directors would appoint all the tag, rag and bobtail for the sake of their own security. That cannot possibly be beneficial to the welfare of the business."

"Quite right," smiled the official. "In that case no reasonable business could exist, but just because this is so, it follows as a matter of course that the managers have no need to fear public opinion when they can truly answer to their consciences for their decisions. For since every Freelander knows that freedom in the choice of a business is the foundation of our organization in the form of companies, he also knows that the sensible and orderly management of all the companies is the foundation of all our wealth. And since the prosperity of each company lies in the immediate interest of everyone on account of the freedom which we have in choosing our business, thus making it possible for everyone to obtain the post where he receives the best remuneration, so everyone has an immediate interest in shunning everything which could disturb this thriving arrangement. Thus frivolous interference in the right of managing the conduct of the business is also avoided. No Freelander would consent to take your part against a manager who does not employ you according to your wishes. You might make a great noise in the newspapers about it, and you may even succeed in making a number of persons believe that your director has not a right idea of your talents. But even those who believe you will say that it is not proper for them to judge the manner in which such questions are settled. Even if the opinion should get abroad that the director in question is quite unfit to estimate the talents of those who are under his management properly, yet no workman who is outside the company in question will presume to wish to interfere, since he will say that watching over the fitness of a manager is the exclusive business of the workmen who are employed in that particular company. In short, in order that the public opinion of Freeland should interest itself on your behalf, it is not only necessary to prove that a mistake has been committed, but that the business is conducted in a malicious manner and that the majority of your fellow workmen are also guilty of this malice. In such cases public opinion first examines the facts, and gives the decision afterwards in a general assembly of the company which has been accused of such conduct, and everyone is present at this assembly who has an interest in the matter."

Beside this, the official told me that I should obtain more detailed information about everything that was necessary for the choice of my future profession from the reports of the Central Statistical Office, which were kept everywhere, and were also lying in the free reading rooms and libraries, and also from the extracts and explanations of the different public notices which were based on these reports. I then departed and as it was close upon dinner time, I went to one of the great restaurants, at which the Freelanders who do not possess a household of their own, or who, for any reasons at all, prefer to take their meals away from home, are accustomed to have them. The restaurants are like the factories, carried on by great companies, and those who have households also supply almost all their wants from this source. The bills of fare are published daily in the newspapers, and the mistress of every house orders by telephone the dishes which she requires. Vans, specially fitted up for this purpose, carry the eatables from house to house, and they assure me that this is not only really cheaper, but also far better than cooking at home.

I was immediately convinced of this. The food was prepared entirely from the choicest ingredients, and the price is only half of what one has to pay for a similar meal at a European restaurant. This cheapness is of course partly due to the fact that in Kenia the raw materials are fabulously cheap on account of the indescribable luxuriancy of nature. But it is also explained by their preparation at a proportionately low price through large quantities being operated upon at once, notwithstanding all the labor that is expended upon them. I learnt that a kitchen manager, five overseers, and twenty employees can cook enough in one day for twenty-seven thousand persons. Of course they have machines and apparatus for assisting them in their work, far surpassing anything used in the great English and American hotels. They cost a great deal, but what does that matter in comparison with the great saving of labor which they effect, and especially here where human working power is the most precious of all things!

When I had dined, a waiter brought me my bill, and when he saw that I was a new arrival who was not yet perfectly acquainted with the customs of the place, he told me I might sign it.

"Why?" I asked.

"As a receipt for the Central Bank."

"Is one fed at the public expense? What has the Central Bank to do with the dinner bill?"

"The bank will naturally put down the amount to your account."

"But I have no account at the bank."

"Then you will open an account with it now, for everyone here has his banking account, in which all he earns is put down to his credit and all he spends to his debit."

"And who pays for me if, for example, I only stop here on my journey through the country, or if I intend to remain here and not do any work?"

"We are quite confident as regards that. Besides I have never yet heard that anyone who has once been in Freeland has ever gone away again, or that an active man has ever refused to work here. If anyone really will not work, we have too much compassion on him to let him die of hunger. And if, for any reason, you do not pay your account, that will be a loss which we shall bear with patience. Nobody in Freeland troubles himself with giving or receiving cash on account of such trifles. Since you do not receive cash anywhere here, no one will ask you for cash payments."

I thanked the man for his information, signed the account, and departed. As it was only two o'clock in the afternoon, and I could not therefore expect to find a manager's office open, I next visited one of the public libraries. It was a large building, in the courtyard of which was a noble pleasure garden into which all the reading rooms opened. One can sit sometimes in the open, and sometimes in covered places, and I at once perceived by the great crowd, which was partly reading and partly talking, that the inhabitants of Freeland have a predilection for using their libraries as public meeting places for the exchange of ideas and for many kinds of amusements. There is the greatest silence on one side of the rectangle which encloses the court-yard, as the student's saloons for the use of that part of the public which does not come here for amusements, but for study, are situated there. But there was the most lively bustle everywhere in the pleasant and lofty saloons, and in the shady garden which was separated from them by a colonnade.

I asked in which saloon the written details of the departments of technical employment lay, and was soon deeply engaged in what was to me the most interesting occupation, that of comparing the last returns of the various workshops of the country. At the same time I immediately perceived that the journals in their articles have regard to the needs of those learned in technical science as well as to those of the workmen. Anyone taking an interest in this subject, and having the requisite amount of understanding can, especially if he allows himself to be advised by the materials offered in the reports of the Central Office of Statistics, obtain the minutest information concerning what happens in the sphere of his department of production. For it is a fundamental law of Freeland that any person or company may work at whatever is most profitable, provided that the public is kept informed of all business transactions. The companies are therefore obliged to conduct their book-keeping openly. The prices at which goods are bought and sold, the net profits, and the number of workmen must be communicated at intervals which are fixed according to the judgment of the central office. The information is here sorted and published with such rapidity that I could, for example, see on the tables lying before me how many hours work had been done during the past week by the people occupied in the establishment to which the official of the Central Statistical Office had directed my attention, how many of these altogether spent their time as operatives and apprentices, how many were engaged as inspectors and technicalists, and what is the amount of the pay of each single individual. Deception is totally forbidden, not merely on the ground that everyone has the right to form his decision from what is contained in the books, but because all receipts and expenditures go through the Central Bank which is in connexion with the Office of Statistics. Thus the communications demanded by this last enable a double control to be exercised over those extremely important statements which are the foundation of the organization of labor in Freeland.

Every working man can understand from the table of statistics at a glance where he can at that moment get the greatest amount of pay. Of course this is not everything, for this highest rate of pay is sometimes coupled with circumstances which may not please everyone. Life may be tedious in the particular district, or the opportunities of educating children may not be so many as elsewhere in Freeland. This is sufficient to prevent the workmen of Freeland who are not in difficulties from selling their services for a high price, and from making use of such opportunities of work, even if some hundreds of shillings more may be made in a year by the same amount of exertion. But it follows as a matter of course that information on this point is also to be obtained in the reports. The prospectuses of some of the departments of labor even group the various industrial and rural employments with regard to such details, and, as an example, a report has come before me in which a waving line shows how they are situated at the various places for making money with regard to the profit to be got from the business and nearness to theaters. It follows that since as a matter of fact the highest point in the line of profit intersects the lowest point of the theater line, those workmen in Freeland who at that time obtained the greatest profit were those who have no opportunity of going to theaters. I merely mention this in passing and will not enquire whether it really has anything to do with the modern love of shows, or whether it is only due to chance.

The line of profit which interested me personally, namely that of the mechanical engineers, showed as I was already aware, a depression at the great establishment which was occupied in making railway materials. But as this was not very great, I determined to adhere to my original intention, and join this company, which was called " The First Edendale Engine and Railway Materials Manufacturing Company." In the meantime, it was past three o'clock, and I could at once proceed to settle the matter.

CHAPTER VI.

THE CONSTITUTION OF A MANUFACTURING COMPANY IN FREELAND AND THE PROFIT OBTAINED FROM IT.

THE electric tramway brought me in a few minutes to the huge and complex mass of buildings which the "First Edendale Engine and Railway Material Manufacturing Company" occupies in one of the southern suburbs of Edendale. A signboard showed me the way to the admission office of the company, and a short time afterwards I was in the presence of the manager who had to decide upon the suitability of those who presented themselves.

When I had stated my wish to belong to the company's engineer corps, the manager asked me if I had testimonials or other papers which gave proof of my ability. For this purpose I of course had nothing else than the testimonials of the Academy of Technical Instruction, but these were excellent, and therefore the manager told me, when he had examined them, that they would do, and render it unnecessary for me to be examined as to my abilities, and that he would immediately let me take part in the manufacture of machinery. But I must make myself acquainted with the statutes of the company first, as it is always possible that some paragraph of these may not quite correspond to my expectations. This could naturally, he added, only refer to the regulations for the division of profits, for the statutes of all the companies in the Freeland contain the same principles. But I must carefully read through the pamphlet given me, and sign it, if its contents perfectly agree with what I require.

"To what," I asked, "does my signature bind me when I have given it?"

"Roughly speaking it binds you to nothing or next to nothing. You simply declare thereby your accession to our company and are a member of it from that time. You undertake, as you will see from paragraph 6, some of the responsibility for the loan which has been made to our establishment, yet, as the same paragraph says, only according to the amount of the profits which you receive, and as you only get this according to the amount of the services which you have rendered, you are responsible for nothing as long as you have done no work, and after doing work you are only responsible according to the proportion in which the share of the profits which you obtain from the company stands to the total sum of the profit which all the members have had since the commencement of the debt. The debts which we owe at this time to the Commonwealth of Freeland amount all together to two and a half millions sterling, but the profit which our members have hitherto made since the existence of these debts amounts to almost eight millions sterling, and naturally increases with every day and every hour during which the business is carried on. If you, let us suppose by way of example, leave the company after the space of a month and have obtained sixty pounds sterling as your share of the profits, you are, till the moment you leave, responsible with us for our debt to the amount of twenty pounds, and even if you leave us, this pledge of yours is perfectly extinguished only when our debts which were in existence or contracted while you belonged to our company are quite paid off. Should the undertaking for any reason come to an end before this happens and should the debts not be covered by the sale of the existing machinery and other things pledged for them, you would have to bear your share of it even if you had nothing more to do with us. Your signature always has some material signification even if you are not at the same time pledged to any amount, and the danger of possible future sacrifice which could be imposed upon you if things came to the worst, is a very small one. Yet it is necessary to estimate before-hand in all cases what one is signing, and I therefore repeat my demand that you should carefully read through the copy of the statutes which you have in your hands."

I must confess that in spite of this explanation I did not in the least realize the responsibility which devolved on me immediately on signing the statutes. But since I was, as a matter of course, desirous of being better acquainted with the statutes of a Freeland company, I complied with the request which had been made to me without any further delay. The following are the statutes word for word:—

(1.) Everyone is quite free to join the First Edendale Engine and Railway Material Manufacturing Company, even if he also belongs to other companies. Everyone is also permitted to leave the company whenever he chooses. The board of management decides in what branch of the works the members shall be employed.

(2) Every member is entitled to an amount of the net proceeds of the company corresponding to the quantity of work which he has done.

(3) The amount of work which each member does is calculated according to the number of hours during which he has worked, but with the difference that older members have, on account of their experience, an additional payment of two pro cent. for every year that they have belonged to the company before the others joined. Foremen and founders receive an additional pay of ten pro cent., and night work also receives the same additional pay.

(4) The work which is done by the engineers is paid for as if from ten to fifteen hours work a day had been done, and within this margin the value of each man's work is estimated by the managers. The work of the managers is compensated for by paying them for a number of hours' work done every day, this amount of work being fixed by the general assembly.

(5) Out of the company's profits a deduction is first made towards repayment of capital, and after this the tax to the state is deducted. The remainder is divided amongst the members.

(6) If the company is dissolved or liquidated, the members are responsible in proportion to the amount of profit which they get from the revenues of the company, and this responsibility for the amount which is still pledged is proportionately laid upon the new members. When a member leaves the company, his responsibility for the debt which has already been contracted is not extinguished. In case of dissolution, liquidation, or sale, this responsibility corresponds to the claim of the responsible member to the means of the company which are in hand or to his share in what is sold.

(7) The principal judicial body of the company is the general assembly, in which every member has the same right to speak and exercises the same active and passive right of choice. The general assembly makes its determination by simply counting the majority of votes. A majority of three quarters is necessary for changing the statutes, and for a dissolution, or liquidation of the company.

(8) The general assembly practises its right either directly or by means of its chosen officials, who are answerable to it for their actions.

(9) The business of the society is managed by a directorate of three members who hold this office at the will of the general assembly. The subordinate functionaries are chosen by the managers.

(10) The general assembly selects every year a committee of inspection which consists of five members. This body has to control and make a report upon the books and the manner in which the company is conducted.

What at once astonished me in these statutes was the want of all information regarding the wealth of the company. Since this wealth is well known to consist of the plant which has been gotten together with the help of the money borrowed from the state, and as it is the members who pay this capital with sums which are deducted from the net proceeds, it appeared to me to be only just that the said wealth should belong to the members, as I told the manager.

"You are mistaken," he replied, "the payments on account of the capital of the company are not made by the members, but by the consumers. It is therefore clear that the amount of the capital which is used upon every piece of goods produced is added on to the price. If this were not so, the members would have less than the profit corresponding to the average value of labor in Freeland, and the evident result would be that in such a case a large amount of working power would leave the company. The supply of the articles in question would be diminished, and their price would consequently go up until the balance was restored. Besides, there is nothing in this peculiar to Freeland. In the *bourgeois* world also, the amount sunk in machines, tools, and other contrivances necessary for the production of a piece of goods is reckoned up in the price, and the difference between Freeland and the rest of the world consists only in the fact that the process of the free movement of workmen, and the equalization of net profits which is thereby rendered more easy and more perfect, are accomplished much more surely and completely here than elsewhere. The throwing off of the payment of capital on to the consumers is only rendered impossible if the company has procured bad or unnecessary machines which are either not required for producing the goods which the company manufactures or for supplying the needs of these machines, or which ought not to be used for these purposes at all. The public does not pay for such machines, the members must do that. Therefore they see their share in the profits sink below the full value of labor through the capital being paid off. But such machines are, on account of this, unnecessary, and must be sold. If this is done, the responsibility of the members for the loss which has arisen in this manner really comes into existence now for the first time, for, as paragraph 6 says, they have exceeded their means. Therefore the loss which arises from the sale is put down to their account. But as long as the capital, that is, the means, is actually at work, nobody has any right to interfere with our arrangements, but everybody according to his liking should be engaged in the kind of employment which corresponds to his abilities."

I was satisfied on this point, and proceeded now to a discussion of those provisions of the statutes of the company which immediately concerned myself.

"I suppose," I said "that you will place me as a new comer

in the lowest rank of engineers, and my days' work will equal the work which an ordinary laborer does in a day of ten hours. According to the statistics which I have already examined, the pay of ordinary work has lately averaged five shillings an hour. I shall therefore at the highest get fifty shillings a day. In what form, and how often shall I be paid? Will it be daily, weekly, or monthly? I am aware that no one gives cash payments here; perhaps I receive bills on the Central Bank from the treasury of the company?"

"We have no treasury here, and you receive nothing from us for the value of the work which you have done. All that we have to do with the payments is that we punctually inform the bank every week of the amount of work which our members have done. There the amount which you have earned is put down to your credit, and in the same manner the amount which you spend in supplying your wants is communicated to the Central Bank. It keeps your accounts, and sends you an abstract every week."

"But what about the number of hours' work that I perform. Perhaps at first ten, while later on I shall do more. How long, as a matter of fact, have I to work?"

"Six hours a day, from nine to twelve in the morning and from three to six in the afternoon. No work is done on Sundays, and we have besides fifteen various holidays. You have, like every other inhabitant of Freeland, two months' holidays a year, and you have to arrange with your colleagues as to the time of year when these are taken. No one is compelled to have holidays, for since permission is not given to all to go at the same time, but only in suitable batches, anyone having no need or no desire for holidays can go on working. Payment naturally ceases during holidays. One is paid, however, except when one has a right to be maintained at the public expense, only for services which have been rendered."

"You would not consider it rude of me," I said, "if I asked you according to what principle your pay, and that of the other members is fixed? Are there no settled rules, or can you ask what you please?"

"What I demand for my pay is wholly dependent upon myself, and what my colleagues demand is wholly dependent upon themselves. But the general assembly have the sole power of granting this."

"And is not your dependence in this point on those whom you manage connected with some inconveniences. Does not discipline suffer from it?"

"How so? The general assembly granted me my pay, which amounts to twenty-five hours' worth a day, not according to caprice or favor, but according to necessity, and, therefore, according to that which the members think to be useful and necessary for their own interest. I receive as much as the members of the company must pay to get the man whom they require to conduct the management. It is quite possible that they have erred on one side or the other concerning my fitness, either by valuing me too much or not enough, but I depend upon their estimate of my fitness, and not upon their favor. The pay of managers depends, as all other economical matters in Freeland do, exclusively on offer and demand. Do you think then that your pay is about twice as much as that of an ordinary workman, because someone might think of giving you more than the others? If we kept people of your capacity to the same pay as ordinary workmen, they would have to be contented with it. Your power is of a more rare kind, but it is more sought for, therefore you will be paid what is necessary. It is exactly the same in my case. Were people of my learning and experience as common as ordinary operatives, I should have to be contented with the pay of an operative."

"But," I remarked, "in this case you would still prefer undertaking the business of management to performing ordinary manual work. I would also prefer my duties to those of an operative, even if I did not get any more money, and I believe that it would, on that account, be quite possible to settle all differences of income if it were only made a fundamental law that as regards division of profits nobody should receive any more than the rest."

"This is altogether erroneous," he replied. "In that case you have given the same amount of profit to various degrees of ability, and not to various degrees of industry, or perhaps you think it necessary to make the idle and industrious equal? Would you do any good by mechanically measuring pay according to the number of hours of work? Who would then do the harder and more disagreeable kind of work without compulsion? Or do you prefer such compulsion to inequality? You shake your head. Why then would you place the wise and foolish on the same level by means of compulsion? But, supposing that this were just, it is impossible, without injuring the welfare of all in such a manner that the unskilful would be much worse off than they are under the present system of inequality. I see before all things that the skilful would hardly seek appointments corresponding to their abilities if nothing were to be gained thereby, for we do not consider ordinary hand labor to be at all disgraceful. At any rate a higher material advantage is the surest means of placing a man in that position in which he can be of the greatest use. Lastly, there are even various honorable posts, and I, for instance, do not know, as far as I am concerned, whether I should prefer a professor's chair to my present post of manager. But it appears that my capacity for organization has a better value here than it would there, and the greater pay which our company has assured to me is the only thing that keeps me in the position where I am required. Be that, however, as it may; Equality introduced by compulsion is at any rate contrary to the principles of Liberty. With what right shall the state forbid that a society of free men shall divide the produce of their work among one another in such a manner as it thinks to correspond best to its interests, as long as it does not thereby violate any right? My companions found that it is to their advantage that I should be their chief. Who can hinder them from giving me an advantage because I, on my side, take every care of their interests?"

As it evidently seemed to please my friendly chief to dissipate my doubts, I took courage to ask him yet another question.

"I can quite understand after what I have heard that differences are also made between the work done by ordinary workmen, and there is nothing further to remark about the additional payments which are given to overseers and foremen who have to perform either heavier or more fatiguing work than others. I therefore understand that night work, in so far as it is generally needed, must be more highly paid, otherwise no one would undertake it, but a danger appears to me to lie in the additional payments to elder men, which can hardly be thus justified. Since the statutes, as I am aware, are made in the general assembly, it lies in the power of every workman to put this additional payment very high in order to render the addition of new workmen more difficult. In our state, two pro cent. is added for every year, and this is at any rate justified by the increase in the experience and aptitude of a workman during a year, which may be valued at two pro cent. A man who has been with us for twenty years receives about fifty pro cent more than the new comer who is working at his side, but no question arises in this matter, for he does more work in proportion. But supposing our workmen were suddenly able to fix the increase of pay on account of age from two to five or perhaps ten pro cent. or more a year. Then a man who has been here ten years would get twice as much as if he had been here twenty years. He would get three times as much as a new comer whose ability was equal to his in other respects, and that would in my opinion have the same effect as if our workmen had determined to receive no new comers. Who hinders our self-governing workmen from taking such a determination?"

"No one," was the answer. "It is quite likely that in one of our next general meetings such a decree might be made. Yet you may rely on the fact that it would not remain in existence for long ; for just in the same manner as a general meeting which is summoned one morning can determine that the additional payment for long service should amount to ten pro cent. a year, a general meeting summoned the next morning could repeal this decree, and you can easily guess what sort of a majority it would be which would determine upon this repeal. The power of joining any company in Freeland also offers defense against these excesses of unbounded egoism. It also lies in the interest of older workmen not to measure the additional payment on account of age so high that the addition of new workmen should be checked thereby. The additional payment on account of age has an intention and signification if it confers an advantage upon those who enjoy it over others who either do not yet receive it or do not receive the same amount of it. If we suppose that a million is to be divided amongst a thousand members, it is exactly the same to them whether they determine that everyone shall receive one unit or two units. In the first case, the unit will be a thousand, in the latter five hundred. If the sum to be divided has grown in proportion to the admission of new members, it means that the older men entitled to a share in the proceeeds have an advantage. The older workmen already see that their own interest does not lie in opposing the public estimation of what is a just and suitable value of their rights.

"We have now talked sufficiently, and I will introduce you to the chief of your future office, and you can begin to work to-morrow if it is convenient for you to do so." Saying this, my friendly chief rose and invited me with a wave of his hand to follow him.

CHAPTER VII.

WHY FREELAND USES SO MUCH MACHINERY AND WHENCE IT OBTAINS IT.

WE walked through a row of passages and at last entered the workroom of the chief engineer of the establishment. This man seemed to me to be one with whom I must have been very familiar a short time before, but his beard and exterior person did not quite come back to my memory again, so I did not know who he was. But he recognized me immediately, and, seizing me by the arm with a cry of joy, said to the director " This is the same Robert N. whose enthusiasm it was, as I have repeatedly told you, that first made me long for social liberty and finally made me come here. It is now four years since we took leave of one another at the Polytechnic. He has not changed in the least, but I have become so thoroughly a Freelander that he did not at first recognize me."

The manager, who thought his presence no longer necessary, soon took his leave with a few cordial words, and I remained alone with my friend. " I have already been expecting you for a long time," he said turning towards me. " I was quite confident that you would come, and I have systematically examined the alphabetical lists of new comers as well as those in which they are arranged according to their professions and the places that they come from. You will of course leave the place where you are staying immediately and be our guest until you have made further arrangements. I must tell you that I have been married for two years. I will say nothing about my wife now, you will see her presently. Let us despatch our business at once, and then go home as quickly as possible to my Vera, who has been desirous of knowing you for some time. You must now be presented to your colleagues, and then make a short inspection of the workshops. But stop, I had almost forgotten to order your luggage to be sent from the hotel to our dwelling. Your hotel is—?"

I gave the name, and heard my friend, we will call him by his christian name Charles, telephone the order about the removal in question. I thought that it was superfluous affectation to raise objection to this proceeding, in the face of the fact that we had once been warm friends, and that this friendship did not appear to have cooled during the interval.

I will not dilate any further upon the reception which I obtained from my present colleagues, but will only remark that their exceptional and evidently sincere cordiality surprised me very agreeably. When I made a remark on this to Charles, he took me laughingly by the shoulder and said, "Yes dear brother, we are now in Freeland. Why should not young men be pleased at receiving a colleague who has it written in his face that he is a fine fellow? Need any one here fear that he will be kept short on your account? Must they perceive in you an influential person who will prevent them from being promoted? It may indeed happen that one or the other will say, 'He appears to me as if he would succeed better than I.' But what harm would that do to them? The more able you are, the better it will be for all. Here you will have no enemies, for you will have no occasion of doing any harm to anyone."

What filled me with astonishment as we entered the workshops was less their size than the accomplishment of mechanical operations with every care for the convenience, health, and safety of the workmen. There are also, it is true, equally great works in Europe, but there are none outside Freeland in which mechanical power so greatly increases and takes the place of human power. The apparatus which I saw here bore comparison with the best that I had known up to that time and which was used, like this, for making machinery. Man was in truth here only the overseer who watched over and guided the labor of the elements.

Upon a remark which I made to Charles regarding this, he replied. "That is quite natural; they cannot have these perfect machines in Europe because there would be no demand for them, exactly for the same reason that, for example, there would be no demand for an English or French equipment in China. What are machines then? They are the products of past labor with the help of which present and future labor will be economized. In Europe there is a significant difference between the worth of the product of labor and that of the working power, for the present and future labor which will be saved by the machine receives only bare wages, whilst to the machine, the product of past work, there are attached the profit to the owner, ground rent, and interest on capital, besides the wages which have already been expended in manufacturing it. This difference does not exist with us. Here the day's work which I save has exactly the same worth to me as a day's work which the machine requires for its manufacture, for both are worth as much as the product which has been manufactured, and the employment of that machine is therefore profitable to me which is in general practically useful, that is, which saves more human working power than it requires for its manufacture. But in Europe only those comparatively small machines are necessary which save so much more labor that through this saving the difference in value of the past and future labor is accumulated in the crystallized form of wares. This machine costs twelve thousand pounds sterling, and must be liquidated within ten years; therefore it takes twelve hundred pounds sterling per annum, but it replaces the work of ten men, and is therefore highly useful to us, for ten inhabitants of Freeland, even if they were quite ordinary operatives, would ask for at least three hundred and fifty pounds per man, and thus all together would require three thousand five hundred pounds sterling per annum. Consequently the machine saves us a clear two thousand three hundred pounds. Workshops of the same kind in Europe cannot, on the contrary, use these machines. They would become bankrupt if they did so, for they could not possibly spend twelve hundred pounds sterling per annum, to save the wages of twelve European workmen, since the wages of these ten workmen would, according to the European standard, amount at the most to from six hundred to seven hundred pounds sterling per annum, and it is not practicable to employ twelve hundred pounds to save from six to seven hundred pounds. It is naturally still worse in China; there it is not possible to employ from sixty to seventy pounds per annum to save the expense of ten laborers, for the wages of ten laborers for a year amount to from sixty to seventy pounds sterling.

That that may correspond to what really exists, I must add, as this point of view generally explains, why just the lands with the most miserable wages in the great manufacturing industries possess the least fitness for competition. It is evident that the law which my friend here explained to me must be right. But I still believed, for the sake of perfect explanation of the matter as it stood, that I could make the objection, that, as it appeared to me, lands with high wages must find machines dearer than those with cheap wages. The machine, I thought, is itself the product of human work, and where this work is highly paid, anything manufactured by it must also be dearer.

"The contrary is the case," replied Charles. "First of all I beg of you to think that, as I have already observed, ground rent, interest on capital, and profit must be added to the price of the machine in Europe besides the wages. You must pay rent to the owner of the ground upon which metal and coal are mined and timber felled, for permission to perform these operations. You must pay interest to the capitalist for the capital that has been necessary to make these machines, and besides this interest pay or charge to yourself the capital which has been expended upon these machines, and finally the enterpriser, the so-called giver of work, will, in Europe, have his profit. These various additions to the wages are proportionately greater, the less the latter additions are, and that explains why the products of countries where wages are small are, on the average, not cheaper than those of the countries where wages are high. The value of the product is the same in both, but their value is divided between workmen and employers in another proportion. The latter receive more when the former are contented with less."

"So you believe," I asked, interrupting my friend, "that the moneyed classes in the countries where there are moderate wages are better off on that account than they are in those countries where wages are high? That seems to me to be contrary to what actually exists, because in China, for example, the moneyed classes are poorer than they are in England."

"Quite right," answered Charles. "And it follows from this that much more is produced in England than in China. Landlords, capitalists, and enterprisers certainly get more out of single manufactured products in China than in England, but for every product which they produce and consume, ten can be produced and consumed in England. And this is immediately seen to follow as a matter of course, if one only remembers that workmen who are ten times better paid consume ten times more, and that tenfold consumption presupposes tenfold production. And because they obtain a proportionately smaller share in the profits, but from a fourfold greater amount of goods, the moneyed classes in England are richer than those of China. And this is not more than what inevitably follows, if one considers that every possession of the moneyed classes consists, as a matter of fact, in the ownership of the means of production, and that wherever the masses consume more, the rich necessarily own more means of production.

"Now let me continue where you interrupted me. There is, as a rule, no moneyed class with us in Freeland which lives by the amount of the net proceeds which it keeps away from its workmen, and the price of the manufactured goods need not be higher here on that account. But what is more, it can, as a rule, be even lower, and this in spite of the fact that our working men not only get as much as the laborers and capitalists together do in Europe, but really more. For exactly the same thing that happens in the case of goods which we manufacture here with the help of machines, namely, that we can use much more and more important machinery for producing them than is possible in Europe, exactly the same thing happens even in the manufacture of the machines themselves; they would also be made by using far more and more important machine power than would have been possible in Europe. As I have told you, this machine costs twelve thousand pounds sterling. It was bought two years ago, and at that time the average yearly wage of the workmen of Freeland was three hundred pounds sterling. It, together with the raw materials and plant necessary for its manufacture, has also been the amount produced in a year by forty Freeland laborers. In Europe one would have thought a greater amount of expenditure of labor to be necessary for this purpose, and you see that these machines can be sold cheaper here than in Europe, although the workmen employed in making them get four times the amount which the workmen, owners of ground, capitalists, and enterprisers together get in Europe. Our manufactured goods are, on the average, much cheaper than those made in Europe, but we produce very much more, and all that we produce belongs to us, the workmen."

After we had walked through a row of workshops, my friend asked me to leave the establishment by the back door, instead of by the principal entrance, as he would then see on the way whether all his orders were punctually executed in the enlargements and new buildings which were then in course of erection

"We are about to enlarge our premisses," he added by way of explanation.

When we arrived at the site of the buildings, the many mechanical aids, in Europe altogether dispensed with, which I saw everywhere employed by builders and stone-masons astonished me. The bricks were conveyed upon electric railways, raised by electric cranes straight out of the waggons to the various storeys, and there brought to the workmen by an automatic machine, so that some had only to control the machines while others did the building. I was at once impressed by the grandeur of the new buildings. "We are spending a large amount of money on these," I said to Charles, "and the state finds it all. Where does the state get the necessary sum from?"

"From the produce of our taxes, dear friend," he replied. "Last year six hundred and fifty thousand workmen of Freeland produced goods to the value of three hundred and sixty millions sterling, and of that the state has kept not less than one hundred and twenty-five millions sterling for its own purposes. The companies have also paid about twenty millions for the loans received in former years, so that altogether one hundred and forty-five millions have flowed into the coffers of our state. Naturally cnly a part of the sum can be had for new projects, as the state has also to fulfil its own obligations. But you perceive that something can be had out of such an amount."

"Of course," I replied. "But as I know that every company has the right to ask for as much as it wishes, it is not yet clear to me how sufficient is found, even with such giant sums as these, for wishes are boundless, and all revenues have a limit, although it may be a very wide one."

"Certainly," answered Charles. "Wishes are boundless, but only when one does not have to pay for them. Capital is not given to us, but only advanced, without interest indeed, but to be paid back again."

"How easily you silence me!" I replied. "You will certainly not ask for any capital for irrational purposes, at least you will not intentionally do so, since it has to be paid back. But that machine which saves human work, as you have just explained to me, is in demand in this country, and if I can ask as much as I like, I promise to use the one hundred and forty-five millions of pounds of your yearly revenue for one great establishment."

"You had better let that remain as it is, my good friend," laughed Charles. "You forget the small detail that appliances and machines, in order to be in demand, must not only save labor, but must also find a sale for the products which are obtained by their means. Would you allow this new building to be erected if you did not calculate that the goods which will be manufactured would sell. Ask the millionnaires and milliardaires in Europe and America if they would build everything for which they have capital, and you will receive the answer that it is altogether impossible, because they must be guided in their plans by the sale of goods. Now only a few of these clever fellows know that the sale is so pitiably small, and must remain so as long as civil order is not uprooted, because the proletariate masses of the world derive no advantage from increasing productiveness, and so their wages, that is, their power of buying, cannot be increased. Purchasing power increases with us proportionately with every improvement in productive power, but it is not on that account less true with us that production can only increase *pari passu* with demand and that therefore appliances for the products of which there are no purchasers would be useless. What is even more, this harmony between increase of sale and production is much more perfect with us than it is with the rest of the world For there the speculators, just because they do not know what they ought to do with capital, often go in for schemes which nobody makes any use of, in the hope that they will succeed in driving away customers from their rivals. If there are many such speculators, a crisis is the result. This is not possible with us, for here no one can demand or establish unnecessary undertakings, because no one is puzzled as to how he shall employ his capital. Here we only set up such works as will produce things that are likely to be in demand, and the buyers of these naturally fall off if the capital requisite for setting up the business exceeds the means of the state, because in this case the business must be carried on at the cost of the consumer, and such an undertaking tends to produce more because one requires less."

"So you prevent," I asked, "every possibility that more could be demanded for the purposes of business than it is generally possible to obtain? How does it come to pass then that in the rest of the world the rate of interest sometimes becomes so enormous? Is it not caused by the demand of capital at times exceeding the supply? You will not deny that this increase in the rate of interest frequently occurs in Europe and America and puts an end to the further increase in the demand for capital, thus bringing the supply and demand for capital into equilibrium. We do not possess this safety valve in Freeland, how shall I explain that in spite of this fact the equilibrium between supply and demand in the capital market cannot be disturbed, but that here under all circumstances the employment of that capital which is to be disposed of must be demanded. For if it is impossible to demand more capital than is to be obtained, it is also impossible to demand less. If, on the one hand, I ask whether the ability of our state to lend capital could be lessened by a large demand for it, the question arises on the other hand what we shall do with the unemployed surplus if less capital is demanded?"

"I will first answer the question with which you concluded, because then an answer will as a matter of fact be given to all earlier questions. We can never have more capital than is likely to be required because the collection of our capital is not allowed to take place by chance, but is systematically undertaken by the state in the form of an imposition of taxes. The amount of this tax is, from the nature of what is collected, not immutable, and it follows therefore that the tax is always adjusted to satisfy all the needs of the public, who also have the right of disposing of the capital. Our bodies of representatives base their calculations concerning the probable demand on the information which they get and on principles learnt by experience, and adjust the amount of the tax accordingly. This method is, of course, liable to errors, the amount received in one year exceeds the demand by some millions, and in another year it is below the demand. But the result of such disparities is only that in the first case the excess is carried on to the next year, and in the second case that part of the enterprises is put off for some weeks. Too much capital to be disposed of is also impossible, since it is quite evident that we never ask for more than we need."

"Permit me to interrupt you for a moment," I said. "I perceive that our Freeland state never has, if we do not regard transitory disparities, more capital to dispose of than is needed. But capital can be accumulated in the hands of individuals. What is done with the money which is earned but not spent?"

"That only concerns these individuals, since he who earns more than he can or will use can determine himself what he will do with the excess. He will give it away, in which case another, the person to whom he gives it, will spend it, or he will let it accumulate, in which case he will put it by to be spent at some other time. He can also, if he chooses, even use it for speculating with in a foreign country as long as there is such a foreign country, that is, as long as all the world has not taken to our social organization. Private savings do not have anything whatever to do with our money market, for since the demand for capital as it generally exists is supplied by the state without interest, nobody would gain anything by lending capital here, and no one parts from his possessions without gaining something by doing so. There are indeed a kind of private savings which are placed on the capital market in the same manner as the produce of the general taxation. This is the case with the payments made to our insurance office, as you will find out presently. But exactly because this establishment which is managed by the state employs its premiums to cover a part of the capital which is demanded, these premiums are taken into consideration in making calculations concerning the public money in the same manner as the proceeds from taxation, that is their probable amount is deducted when the amount of taxation is fixed upon. Therefore supply in our money market can under no circumstances exceed the demand. In this manner is the question principally answered why there can be no dearth of capital with us as happens at times in the rest of the world. For consider well that even there dearth of capital is only an occasional phenomenon, caused by the circumstance that the accumulation of capital which is left to chance, does not, according to the times, exactly correspond with the demands which it has been intended to supply. We do not allow capital to accumulate by chance, and therefore if the demand increases, we accumulate more capital and therefore raise the taxation in a corresponding manner.

"Finally, I must guard against what I have said meaning that it is quite impossible that with us more capital would be needed than the state could supply. Of course it is true that machines for the products of which there were no consumers are unnecessary, and are therefore not in demand. But it is also true that the manufacture of machines for the product of which there are consumers presupposes the existence of a certain amount of wealth. And the question therefore always arises whether the first or second limit to raising capital is to be considered. If I wish to build a workshop, I have to consider on the one hand whether I can reckon on consumers for the products which I manufacture, and I shall certainly not build if there are no such consumers. On the other hand, I shall have to think where I shall get the capital for my factory from, even if there were consumers for the manufactured products. Which question is now to be considered in practice? For the rich man the first, and for the poor man the second. We are now so rich that the manufacture of all the machines which are really in demand does not trouble us in the least. The worst that a greater exertion of our enterprising powers can lead to is a passing rise in the amount of taxation, and in all circumstances with regard to our affairs the maxim now prevails that taxation has to adjust itself to the demand for capital. At the commencement, when we were still poor, the opposite was the case, for then our means of producing were so small that, by the greatest exertion of our economizing power, we could not make everything that was then wanted at one stroke, but had to adhere to the opposite maxim and regulate our undertakings according to our means of producing."

"And how did you do that?"

"By granting to our administration during the period of transition, that is till the time when our means of producing would have equaled the amount of the need which was felt anywhere for necessary enterprises of capital, the right to choose from among the companies which demanded credit."

"And did not that lead to friction between the companies favored by having capital granted to them and those prejudiced by having it refused."

"No, the freedom of action which exists in Freeland carries in its bosom the true means of safety in such apparent cases of deviation from the common principle of equality of rights. As everyone has the right to join any company that he may please, it was evidently impossible for the companies favored with a grant of capital from keeping the advantage which they derived from it for those who happened to be their members. At first our central government took great care to choose the companies to which credit was to be granted in such a manner that the equalization of the partial increase of production caused thereby should take place as smoothly as possible. It was seen, for example, that if it was in any manner possible, the companies which belonged to the same branch of business were always equally dealt with. This means that as it was not possible to endow, for example, agriculture and the other industries with improved machines at the same time, they did not grant the credit demanded for procuring these improved machines to single husbandmen and artizans, but in the first place only to the husbandmen, and not even to these in such a manner that one agricultural company should at first be perfectly provided with every thing that it wanted, and then that the others should come in their turn, but in such a manner that all should, for example, be first provided with the means for procuring improved plows, and then with the means for procuring improved thrashing machines, and so on. The result of this would be that the articles produced by the favored companies, and in this case we mean agricultural products, would descend in price in such a manner that, while those who were apparently placed at a disadvantage would not increase the amount of goods which they produced, those who were favored could do this, but the value of the goods produced in each case remained the same. If a pair of shoes, for example, had, at the time we are speaking of, the value of one hundred-weight of corn, whilst both needed a day's work for their production, the cobbler received two hundred-weight for his pair of shoes because they required a day's work, whilst, in the case of agriculture, two hundred-weight of corn required a day's work for their production. But this method of equalization was not thoroughly efficient. It was not possible to prevent it from being disturbed by the influence of foreign commerce on the price, and just as little could the principle of dealing equally with all the companies which were connected with the same branch of business be strictly adhered to. Here the influx and efflux of working power was at first of great assistance. But this means could not, under all circumstances, give perfect help, at least, not without thereby very sensibly prejudicing the advantage derived from the machines employed in the work. We could not, for example, when the employment of electric power was determined upon, in the third year after Freeland had been founded, possibly undertake this at one time for even the whole of the agricultural community, but the agricultural companies necessarily had to be supplied in turns. If I recollect rightly, the company of the upper Tana was the one which first received the electric power which was obtained from the great waterfall of the Kilolumi. That placed it in the position to produce in this territory with two thousand workmen as much as had been produced with four thousand. But in order to make the utmost use of this advantage, they must find a means of inducing the two thousand workmen whom they no longer required to go elsewhere. They could not compel them to do that. They need not of course have been idle if they had remained, the superfluous working power would have been used to plow four times where before the ground would have been plowed twice, to till the fields more carefully, and so on, but it is clear that not much would be gained by doing this. Further, since the four thousand agricultural laborers of the upper Tana would, in consequence of the employment of electric power, have always earned more or worked less than the agricultural laborers in other companies, that would have attracted a new addition of labor there until the produce of the labor had sunk through this new addition to the amount obtainable in Freeland at that time without the aid of electric power. This common average would indeed have been fixed at a higher figure, since the laborers who had remained in the other companies would have been able to produce more than before both pro man and per hour, but this increase would have in no wise been so great as the amount of work which was lavished in the other place. To obviate this, there was no other means than that the people of the upper Tana should of their own free will strive to divide the profit which they have made by employing electric power between themselves and the other agricultural companies. The other favored companies followed the same example in the order in which they received the favors, which they perceived were one-sided until the favoring ceased. Some industries preferred to hand over the excess which was obtained in this manner to the state, but the state had no cause to interfere at all in this process of compensation, since it lay in the original interest of the companies which received their share not to retain more of the advantage that was assigned to them than was possible without a combination which would disturb the supply of workmen.

"We also had a time when we could not respond to every application for capital. That was when the equipment with labor-saving machinery was yet to be perfected, and it was just on that account that our power of producing was very limited. Our equipment with labor-saving machinery is nearly finished now, and we have only to improve and complete this machinery, which has immeasurably increased our power of producing.

"When you observe that we of the ' First Edendale Engine and Railway Material Manufacturing Co.' are now on the point of laying out three quarters of a million pounds sterling on buildings, machines, and tools, you may rely on it that we do not do this because three quarters of a million has been advanced to us without interest in the same manner as the rest of our capital, but because the commissions, some of which we have already received, while the remainder are to be expected with certainty in consequence of the great increase of business everywhere in the state, imperatively demand such new works. Now let us go home."

CHAPTER VIII.

A HOUSEHOLD IN FREELAND AND THE RIGHT OF MAINTENANCE.

THE electric tramway conveyed us to Edendale with lightning-like rapidity, and as my friend Charles had chosen his house with regard to the greatest possible convenience of communication, our car set us down just in front of it. A few seconds later the lady of the house, who had evidently been expecting the arrival of her husband by the electric railway, hastened to meet us. The introduction did not take long, and as Charles had, as a matter of fact, spoken to his wife very often about me, we were soon good friends.

We entered the house, and the various rooms were shown to me, including those which had been appointed for my use. "I took care," said Charles, "in laying out the building, for any fresh addition to my family, and we therefore have an excess of room now, since this fresh addition is confined to a boy fourteen months old. You also have a bed room, besides a bath room, a reception room, and a garden terrace for your exclusive use."

It now suddenly occurred to me that there are no servants in Edendale, and I began to entertain scruples as to whether I might not be a burden to my host. But the excuses which I made on this point to Mrs. Vera had the misfortune not to be understood by her.

"Robert," explained Charles ironically, "appears to

apprehend that either you or I will have to brush his clothes."

I protested warmly against this explanation of my thoughts, and not without some satisfaction at the information which I had obtained at the hotel regarding this point. "I can quite imagine," I observed, "that those appointed by the company for rendering personal services will execute the clothes cleaning in private houses. But one may happen to require other services; how can such be obtained?"

"In the same way in this case as at the hotel. You ring, and within two minutes at the most a serviceable sprite awaits your orders."

"And where does this serviceable spirit remain before the bell is rung in order to come so quickly?"

"In one of the waiting rooms which the company which you have mentioned maintains in all parts of the town. All the bells of every house in Edendale are in communication with one of these. Every room has its electric bell, and if a bell is rung anywhere, an apparatus in the waiting room shows the number of the house, and another apparatus in the antechamber of every house shows the number of the room in which the bell was rung. Your ringing will not disturb us and will never even be heard by us. One of the members of the company who is in attendance hastens up on a velocipede, sees the number of your room in the antechamber, and then goes straight to you. Besides, if you are very comfortable, you will not use the bell much. This company attends with great punctuality to every-day wants, such as the cleaning of clothes and rooms, preparation of the bath, which, I may remark in passing, we inhabitants of Freeland are accustomed to have every day, and the bringing of breakfast, dinner and supper, etc., without our troubling ourselves any further about it. I have already informed the committee of management that a new guest has come to my house. One of their officials will come to you in a short time, and subject you to a comprehensive cross-examination as to all your habits, needs, and wishes; if you have once given him exact answers, you may rely that you will be better served here than in any European hotel."

"I must confess that this is wonderful," I replied. "You

obtain the most excellent service in this manner without the domestic miseries which we endure in Europe. But it must be an expensive business, for all these attendants and workmen of the company naturally demand that pay for rendering personal services which is usual in Freeland."

"That is natural," said Mrs. Vera, "but, nevertheless, we do not find their services dear. Last year we paid altogether thirty-two pounds sterling for services."

"How is that possible?" I asked. "It comes to as much as that in Europe for only one servant in spite of the miserable pay."

"Because a European servant," replied Charles, "does everything with his hands, whilst our people do everything by machinery. Some of these machines belong to the household, and others are brought by the attendants of the company when they come. These also sometimes take the things away with them and clean them at their establishment by means of the machines which they have there."

"My dear Madam," I said, "I am quite disposed now to hear that this company, which is present everywhere for the purpose of rendering services, relieves you from the burden of attending to and nursing your children."

"Pardon me," she replied, "but as a rule I attend to that myself. But I am in no wise left to my own resources in this matter, and if I wished, I could get rid of all the trouble. There is, for instance, a company of female nurses especially for the purpose of performing such services at any time for women who have to look for female aid in case of illness or weakness. This company is mainly organized in the same manner as the company for rendering personal services, and has also its waiting-rooms. One can also receive regular services from it, and I need trouble myself no more about my child than, as I know from my childhood, European ladies used to. But this was contrary to my disposition. The company of female attendants had of course a great deal to do in our house until a few months ago, and, if it interests you, I can tell you that the help required in attending to my boy in his first year cost twenty-seven pounds sterling. But these attendants now have almost nothing to do with me. The nursing and attending to my child is my own business."

"Do you carry your child when you go out, or do you push him before you in a perambulator, for even when only fourteen months old, that would make distant excursions somewhat severe!"

"No indeed! What would then be the use of the nursery and kindergarten which are in this neighborhood? When I go out, I take my little one there, where he is well cared for and looked after. But even when I am at home, I let Paul be there very much during the daytime, for even tender mothers will work, read, amuse themselves, and take part in active life, etc., in which children are a disturbance. But I keep him under my own eyes during the greater part of the time."

"You spoke before of the members of the company of female workers. As I know that all women in Freeland have a right to be maintained by the state, why do these women require this kind of profit?"

"Of course every woman of Freeland has the right of maintenance, but no more is paid on account of this right than three-tenths of the average pay of a workman, and there are women who wish to have more. Moreover some are very desirous of being employed somewhere outside their own houses, and as it is not everyone who can effect this by doing brain work, most women have nothing else but the care of children and of those other women who require help. Those women who think that they have the ability for doing brain work prefer the profession of schoolmistress; this, of course, does not prevent them from turning their attention to the other professions."

While we were talking, it struck seven, and an attendant of the food-purveying company appeared and announced that supper was ready.

We repaired to a terrace which led out into the garden where the cloth was laid, and took our places at the table. No food was to be seen until Mrs. Vera opened a cupboard which stood within reach and took out a tureen of steaming soup, and then a cold fish. Vegetables followed these, then roast meat, and then dessert. consisting of cheese and many kinds of fruit. The lady of the house told me that the cupboard also opened from the other side which was in the antechamber and that the dishes brought by the food purveying company were placed in it. This company uses special apparatus for cooling or warming the food, and if customers wish it, certain dishes which are spoilt in being transported, are cooked by the attendants of the company in the house. There are small kitchens with electric ovens in most houses for this purpose, and these can be brought to a glowing heat in a moment in case of need. The attendants of the company also wait at table if required to, but this is very dear, and with the exception of festive occasions, is not usual in Freeland. They feel that the presence of strangers in a circle of friends is always at the least a disturbance.

During supper the conversation again turned to questions concerning women, and especially to the right of maintenance which is granted to women unconditionally. The reader must understand that the second clause of the fundamental laws which have been already laid before him and which states that " Women, children, old men, and those unfit for work have a right to be maintained out of what is produced by the community in a manner corresponding to the common wealth" must be interpreted to mean that a man who has become unfit for either work on account of age or because he met with an accident receives from the state, if a man, four tenths of the average pay for work in Freeland which is calculated from time to time by the statistical office, and if a woman, three-tenths of this amount. Families which have children also get an additional amount of one twentieth of the average pay for each child while he is under age, and this amount is doubled in case of the death of one of the parents, but orphans are entirely taken care of by the state, which nurses and educates them, and this is a privilege which all families enjoy equally. Since the average pay in Freeland was three hundred and sixty pounds sterling in the previous year, each man who is unfit for work gets one hundred and forty four pounds sterling to maintain himself with every woman gets one hundred and eight pounds, and the addition for every child is eighteen pounds if both the parents are alive, and thirty six pounds for the child of a widow or widower. Since the price of all the more important necessaries of life is extraordinarily cheap in Freeland, the real value of these pensions is in fact greater than that of those which European states grant to their best paid officials or to their widows and orphans. They not only suffice to prevent those to whom they are granted from suffering want, but also enable them to share in all those pleasures and comforts which are at the time usual in Freeland and correspond to the amount of common wealth. Since the payments are not made in fixed sums but in amounts corresponding with the rate of wages, they rise with every increase in their wages, and it is in such a manner that those who do no work have their share in the progress of the general prosperity.

When I was about to praise the generosity which was displayed in these arrangements, my friend interrupted me with the remark that in this country no one sees any generosity in a mode of action which is nothing else than the mere fulfilment of a duty, and the recognition of a right which those who are unfit for work have to the general wealth. "That appears to me to go somewhat too far," I observed. "I thoroughly approve, as I have said, that as much assistance as possible should be given to the helpless, but I do not see that all those who work should be obliged to render such help, and that those who are maintained in this manner have a right to their pensions What they get is the produce of the work of others, those able to work have produced it by employing their own energy, and, if they wished to exercise their strict right, they could keep it entirely for themselves."

"Do you really think that?" interrupted Mrs. Vera with flashing eye. "After all that Charles has told me about you, I cannot believe that this is your well considered opinion. You are still evidently being imposed upon by those illusions which are inseparably bound up with the terrible conditions from which you have only just escaped. I have a high opinion of my husband, but it appears to me to be excessive flattery to think that what he produces comes from his own strength, and that the axioms of geometry and algebra which he employs were devised by him, or that the steam engines which he constructs were due to his own inventive genius. I believe that my dear Charles would walk about naked in the forests as a poor savage, if he really had to rely only on that which he might produce with the aid of his own abilities, and I doubt whether any one of us would be in a better position. We are indebted to the previous work of innumerable generations for what we are and what we possesss, and I believe that it follows from this that the stronger and more skilful among us, who alone may be able to deal with the work which has been done by our ancestors, have on that account no exclusive right to the fruits of their work, for this work which they perform only becomes possible with the help of those aids which are the common property of us all. Perhaps you think that Watt invented the steam engine and Stephenson the locomotive only for you and my husband, and not for me and my child, or for the old man and the cripple. Such an idea can only arise in a world which gives the advantage of all inventions to a few privileged persons. Where one sees that the great majority of men are shut out from the enjoyment of the results of increasing productive power, and only receive from those who are the sole possessors of all the wealth of mankind that amount of pay which is necessary for prolonging their wretched existence, and that they make the riches handed down from their forefathers of little use to them, there the idea must of course arise that those who are unfit for work enjoy no right at all. Just so, one only feeds the domestic animals which are profitable, the useless have no claim to shelter and fodder, and if, in spite of this, they do get some, it is only a scanty allowance that is measured out to them. Here everyone has, in case he belongs to the human race, a right to everything that belongs to it. The same principles are followed in Freeland in measuring these rights as are adopted in Europe and America when the usufruct of a rich inheritance is divided among the heirs. Suppose that a man had a factory and left several children, amongst whom some were fit for work and the others unfit, would the first receive the whole inheritance because they alone can cause it to make money by using it? They will want to be compensated for their labor unless they wish to make a present of it to their brothers and sisters, and will demand a larger share; but everyone would think it impudent robbery if they wished to make themselves the only heirs, and their brothers and sisters beggars, to whom they have only to throw alms as a charity."

I confessed with shame to the brave little woman that she had completely conquered me, if the refutation of a prejudice that does not quite agree with one's own principles can generally be termed "conquering." I then added that the extension of equal rights to those who were unfit for work was of great use to the workmen. For want and misery, disgrace and shame are a devouring sore which, eating into the flesh, must at last remorselessly destroy the whole organism, if space is left for it anywhere in the body of society. In the same manner that a family of rank would not endure that disgrace should fall upon one of their members, a whole society, which is in a flourishing state of civilization, cannot endure that anyone of its members should lose his manly dignity. Every one in such a society must keep to his own rights; otherwise the dignity and the rights of others cannot remain safe.

I was rewarded by a look of acknowledgment from Mrs. Vera. But this did not prevent me from bringing forward another question with regard to these pensions which I did not yet quite understand in spite of what had already been said.

"Why," I asked," do all women in Freeland without exception have the right to be maintained? One might even see a degradation of the female sex in this. Can women really produce nothing, and can they consent that such should be supposed of them as a fundamental fact? Perhaps the European ladies are set up as the ideal for women here, those ladies who to be considered as such must prevent even the least suspicion that they are of any use in the world?"

"We women of Freeland wish to make ourselves useful, and we do it too," said Mrs. Vera warmly. "But we think, and our husbands have the same opinion, that nature has in the main assigned a profession to us. In the first place we bear and bring up our children; then we are representatives of what is fine and noble in the state. We are educated for this profession, and we are continually educating ourselves for it. We have the right to go in for any other profession that we please. If we were assigned to these other professions with the idea of securing an independent existence, that would perhaps be very fine in principle, but the greater number of us women would not be in the least useful. Take me as an instance, I could indeed make my living as a designer of patterns, but I should not do it even if I had no right to a pension, for that would suit neither myself nor my husband and least of all my boy. As a matter of fact I should earn nothing, and would be dependent upon the favor of my lord and master. But the worst of the matter is that I should very likely have tried to get my support by being married, and should have looked on marriage as a means of being supported, whilst, on the other hand, relying upon the right of maintenance which I possess in Freeland, I could exclusively follow the dictates of my heart. All the circumstances relating to marriage have also quite a different character with us in Freeland from what they have in Europe. We are not under the guardianship of our husbands, and for that reason we never wish to bring them under petticoat government. European wives are in the main even yet slaves, and if they feel a desire for freedom they must endeavor to get it by employing artifice and round-about ways. They must have their husband's will under their subjection since they dare not have one of their own. It is quite different with us. Here my husband is neither lord, nor does he support me, but is exclusively,"—and here she looked tenderly out of her fine eyes at her husband, finding in his an equally warm response—" my lover, and I believe that this is best, not only for me, but also for him. But this is not all, for the contrary would even be unjust. Can I make my living if I also devote myself to my children and my household? Can I do it all without overburdening myself in a manner with which the men of Freeland are not in the least acquainted? Or is the work which I do as mother and lady of the house less necessary than that which I do by working at a business of my own choosing? But perhaps you will reply that single women can work at a business without overburdening themselves. You are quite right, for a great many women do this, but to wish them to do so would be at the same time imprudent and unjust. Firstly, because the unmarried women would be enticed away from their special profession, and their cultivation would be forced into false tracks, and secondly, because just those women whose education has been carefully conducted and who are suitable for performing women's duties would be condemned to economic dependence. They would have to seek maintenance by being married, and to prevent this, which is a degradation of the finest and most sacred feeling that mankind possesses—namely love—to a matter of gain is the principal purpose of the right of maintenance which exists in Freeland.

CHAPTER IX.

THE CENTRAL BANK, THE MONETARY SYSTEM, THE CENTRAL WAREHOUSE, FREEDOM IN FREELAND.

I HAD entered upon my appointment as engineer in " the First Edendale Engine and Railway Material Manufacturing Company," and soon found that I had fallen into the right place. My way of living was pretty much the same as that of my hosts, and of the rest of the inhabitants of Freeland, but I was quite independent in everything. One generally gets up here soon after sunrise, that is, at about six o'clock, and a cold bath is first of all taken at home. An early breakfast follows, consisting of a cup of chocolate, coffee, or tea, and then a walk either through the streets and magnificent public pleasure grounds of the town, or even on the surrounding hills, which can be reached by an electric railway in ten or fifteen minutes. This walk, which is, as a rule, interrupted by some light reading, is followed by a plentiful breakfast, and then to business. At twelve o'clock one goes home again, or to one of the magnificently-fitted baths which are built on the shore of the Tana and the Lake of Eden. Another repast takes place at one o'clock, but is only a light one, for the principal meal in Freeland takes place in the evening when business is done with. There is sufficient warm meat, cheese, and fruit in the middle of the day, and only very great eaters have more than this. After dinner most of the Freelanders, if they do not prefer a nap, are to be found in the public libraries and reading rooms, those who are married being generally accompanied by their wives, who meet acquaintances, read, and talk about the public events of the evening like the men. Business commences again at three o'clock, and lasts until six o'clock, when those who did not bathe before the mid-day meal have a second bath in the Tana, or in the lake of Eden, and there are even many people who bathe in the morning, afternoon, and evening, a pleasure which is very conducive to health in this warm climate if the various bathings do not last too long. The chief meal is at seven o'clock, and this generally consists of three or four courses. Then the people pay or receive calls, go to the theaters or concert rooms, hear a lecture somewhere, and, in short, attend all kinds of places of amusement or instruction, of which there are plenty in Edendale and everywhere else in Freeland. On Sunday there are special lectures on religious subjects in the morning by pious people, who are consecrated for the exercise of religion, and the afternoon is generally spent in pleasure. Excursions and picnics are arranged, at which music is played, and the young people dance with great zeal.

I naturally preferred to employ my leisure time in inspecting the public institutions of Freeland, among which the Central Bank and the Central Warehouse interested me most. The first is the banking establishment for the whole country, from the government and great manufacturing companies to the last workman, and even to the last child, all of whom have their accounts as I have already related. The bank naturally has branches at every large place in the land. It would be a mistake to think that this universal practice of keeping accounts at the bank needs an especially large staff of employees and requires a great deal of writing. For the very reason that everything passes through the bank the accounts are very easy to keep. Every sum credited to one customer corresponds exactly to a debt of another. No interest is given, and expenditures are of such a uniform kind that the figures have only to be substituted in previously arranged formulæ. The result of this is that seventeen hundred bank officials are required to keep the accounts for the State, for nearly two thousand companies and for two and a-half millions of individuals, and the banking officials are convinced that the process of keeping these accounts will become more simple in proportion as the population increases.

Since no one makes cash payments in Freeland—for I have not seen a single piece of gold except the ready money that I brought with me during the eight weeks that I have hitherto been in Freeland — I wondered at first why the Freelanders always keep the idea of gold before them, and reckon according to it. Their principal coin is the pound sterling, but not the English, which is worth 25 francs and 22·15 centimes, but a pound containing 25 French francs. This pound is divided into 20 shillings, and the shillings into 10 pennies. I explained this matter to myself through the needs of foreign commerce which Freeland carries on with foreign lands to a very considerable extent, but I nevertheless determined to obtain information in a suitable manner, and for this purpose got acquainted with the manager of the bank, who used the same reading room as myself.

This good-natured and somewhat elderly man was very ready to instruct me; and so I learnt as a matter of fact that they have kept gold as money in Freeland because it is the best standard of value, and Freeland is in much greater need of such a standard of value than any other country.

"Is not labor the best standard of value?" I asked. "Do we not exchange things according to the expense of the labor which is necessary to manufacture them? If this book costs five shillings, and that table costs ten shillings, it means nothing else than that the manufacture of them requires the expenditure of as much labor as finding the gold contained in five shillings and ten shillings respectively. Would it not be much more simple to reckon on the amount of work which is expended in manufacturing the book and table directly, to leave money out altogether, and to say, 'This book is worth an hour's work, and the table is worth two hours' work?'"

"I cannot help praising you, my young friend," said the banker obligingly, "for you have, by the exact manner in which you have analyzed the nature of money, made it very easy for me to explain that gold is a good standard of value, while the amount of labor expended is the worst standard conceivable. When we say that the book costs five and the table costs ten shillings, we have not of course assigned to them the value which they were to have in the future, for a book can be worth four shillings just as much as six after the space of a year, and the table can be worth 9 or 11 shilllngs if the proportionate value of the expense of the labor which is required to make a book, table, or shilling should change in the meantime. But if this does happen, we may take it for granted that the cause does not lie in the gold, but in the book or in the table. We can therefore assume that if a book, for example, only costs four marks next year, this is not caused by one hour becoming necessary for the production of four marks which was before necessary for the production of five marks, whilst an hour's labor is necessary for the production of a book at both times. Much rather should we suppose that five shillings of gold can be produced in an hour at both times, but that the expenditure of labor necessary for manufacturing such a book will be diminished by a fifth. And we do not make this assumption on the principle that any mystical quality or constancy of value is inherent in gold, but because the worth of all other things principally depends upon the expense of the labor that is at any time necessary for producing them, whilst, as concerns the value of gold, of which a large amount has been piled up during the course of previous centuries and millenniums on account of its great durability, the influence which is caused by a change in the expense of labor, only takes place slowly in proportion. The value of gold is also at least proportionately more constant than the value of other things; and since it lies in the nature of the matter that one could best use as a standard of value that thing the value of which remains as constant as possible, gold, which is not indeed a perfect measure of value, but is the best that can be obtained under the circumstances, is chosen. That will have become perfectly clear to you with regard to all other things. It does not require much thinking to see that the value of everything is settled in a much better and more secure and enduring manner if one expresses it in a certain weight of gold than if it was expressed in a fixed quantity of any other goods. You evidently possess a less changeable value in a thousand shillings than, for example, in five tons of corn. For next year you will be able to supply all your needs just as well with this thousand shillings as you can now, whilst, if there is a good harvest this year and a bad one next year, these five tons of corn will enable you to satisfy twice as many needs next year as you can now.

"The cost of labor is the worst standard of value possible. For whilst all other things can only possibly change their value, that is, their rate of exchange, according to the total amount of the necessaries of life which are required, it is quite certain that human labor continually changes its value according to the rate of exchange of all the necessaries of life required, and the expenditure of labor required for producing necessaries diminishes as culture increases. For example, if the manufacture of this table requires two hours of labor at the present time, it will perhaps require one and nine-tenths of an hour of labor next year, one and eight-tenths the year after that, and in ten years' time only one hour. And since, as a general rule, the same is the case with regard to all other things, it follows from this that if I owe you one thousand hours' work, this obligation of mine will have its value doubled after ten years, whilst it was the intention of both of us when fixing the amount of the debt to make the advantage and burden of this as unchangeable as possible. And this is best done by fixing the amount of the debt in money and not in hours of work, and not to say 'I owe you a thousand hours' labor,' but to say 'I owe you a thousand shillings.' I will explain this by an example. You are a member of the 'First Edendale Engine & Railway Material Mfg. Co.,' which company is indebted on our books with about two and a-half millions sterling. This debt almost corresponds to the million hours of work according to the price of labor to-day, but at the time when this loan was received, the value of an hour of labor was much less. The erection of the buildings and machines which you now use has consumed more than twenty million hours of labor, because the expenditure of labor required for manufacturing anything is greater the farther back we go from the present time. Would it not be the greatest injustice if it were in general compatible with the existence of your company that it owed and had to pay twenty million hours of labor, whilst, according to the circumstances relating to labor to-day, all their buildings, machines and tools could be made twice over by the expenditure of twenty million hours' labor. And perhaps, after ten years more, twenty million hours' labor would be sufficient to renew that stock four times. Since we reckon in gold, you owe two and a-half millions sterling, and this is about the amount for which your establishment could be renewed to-day, and for which it could probably be renewed ten years hence. A payment can be deferred now and at any future time, but if this does occur, it would only be an accidental deferment against which nothing is done, and which has no special effect. But if there should be any deferment in paying in hours of labor, this would be necessary and lasting; and to build up a payment which is to be made proportional to the value of labor means to designedly ruin the debtors from henceforward.

"But that is not all. The whole of our economy would vanish into air if we wished to fix the value of things according to the cost of the labor expended in producing them. For the first and most important purpose of the standard of value is to measure the value of labor itself. How much the book, table, corn, or iron may be worth is a question of secondary importance; what principally concerns us is to know exactly what is the value of the labor expended on a particular object at any time. If we did not know that, how should we know upon what we ought to expend our labor? The principal question of every economy is that those things should be produced which are needed, and this is accomplished by the workmen turning their attention to those branches of industry in which by the same amount of application they get the greatest amount of produce proportionately to their abilities for the work expended. That means that this table, for example, was manufactured because the ten shillings which it is worth gave the workmen who made it five shillings an hour with which they were contented. They only received these ten shillings for the table, or five shillings an hour, because there was a demand for tables. Had more workmen gone in for table making than corresponded to the demand for tables, the price of tables would have sunk, and the workmen occupied in manufacturing them would have received less than corresponded to the average price of labor. That would have caused them to seek another business for products for which there was a proportionately larger demand, and it is exactly in this manner that equilibrium between supply and demand would be restored. But if the value of the table was expressed not in gold but in the expenditure of the effort necessary to construct it, then these table makers would have received the same price without any change, no matter whether the articles they produced were in demand or not, and this price would be two hours as long as the manufacture of a table took two hours, and only less when the amount of labor which is required for its production sinks, and under all circumstances they would get the same value for the same expenditure of labor, whether what they produce corresponds with the demand or not. Then there remain only two courses open to us; we must either be contented that things be produced which no one needs, whilst there is the greatest want of things which are in demand; or we must use authoritative compulsion in the place of freedom of selection of profession and work. Our courts would then have to determine what should be produced, and this naturally has a further result that the courts must take the whole control of the production into their own hands There is no other means of avoiding that than to supply the free market with a permanently reliable standard of value, that is, with one which is as constant as possible. Such a one is gold, and on that account we have adhered to gold money as a standard of value."

"And why," I asked, "are single payments measured here according to hours of work?"

"Because we wish with regard to such payments as wages, the right to maintenance, etc., that their value should not remain unalterable, but should increase, keeping pace with the increase of production."

I thanked him for the information that I had received, but asked further what is thought in Freeland about that bigoted horror which most of the Socialists of Europe and America have for gold.

"We think that this is only a misunderstanding," he replied. "If gold, or anything else, even the cost of labor, for what I care, were the standard of value, it would remain quite unaffected by those dangers which are predicated of money, but with which we have nothing to do here. Suppose that one wished to reckon in Europe not in money, but in certificates of work, would the power of capitalists be lessened, because they have the power of disposing of so many millions of hours or days of work instead of so many millions of francs or pounds? The evil of the system which obtains in the rest of the world lies in the fact that the workman does not get the full value of what he produces, but the lion's share must be given to the owner of the ground, to the capitalist, and to the owner of the business. Or do the European Socialists believe that if, for example, a hundred-weight of corn should be paid for with ten hours of labor, instead of with ten shillings, these ten hours of labor would belong to the workman who has grown the corn? A change in the standard of value is not in the least necessary to bring this to pass; land and capital must be made accessible to the workman, and the possibility be thus granted to him of working for his own profit. Then the product belongs to him no matter how it is measured, and thus it is thoroughly effected that the value of this belongs to him. The dread of money is like the anger of a child who beats the ground on which he has fallen, thinking that it is the cause of his fall; but let the child once have learnt to walk, and he will stand the more firmly on his feet the firmer the ground is upon which he walks."

I paid a visit with Charles to the Edendale Warehouse to see what these buildings are like in Freeland. In spite of the fact that this business is carried on in one place for the whole country, the warehouse managers maintain special branch dépôts in most places, and these are intended on the one hand for receiving the local produce and sending it to the central dépôt, and, on the other hand, for supplying the local needs out of the produce of the whole country. Foreign commerce goes through the hands of the storehouse administration in the same manner. It may be remarked here that Freeland almost exclusively manufactures those goods for the production of which machinery is principally used, whilst those goods which, on account of their nature, are principally made by hand, are imported from abroad. For if the workmen of Freeland were quite superior as regards work which is done by hand to the enervated workmen of the rest of the world on account of their greater intelligence and physical fitness, in spite of this the handwork which is done in Freeland could not compete with that which is done in the rest of the world on account of its high value, which is, on an average, fifteen times as much as it is in Europe. Our ability to compete first comes into existence when we let our steel slaves take the place of the slaving work of the day laborer of the *bourgeois* world. For these slaves of ours are less costly than the slaves of foreign countries, who at least require to be fed upon potatoes and to be clothed with a few rags, whilst ours are fed by the elements almost without any cost, and a little lubricating oil is sufficient to keep their limbs flexible. In this manner Freeland, in foreign commerce, plays the part of a factory-owner, and foreign lands take the part of a day laborer, and this is exactly the same as what takes place in the foreign commerce of all the lands where wages are different. It is, for example, the English manufacturing industry which produces for China, and Chinese hand labor which produces for England.

The Warehouse of Freeland does not charge the producers anything for storing and selling their wares. The fees are paid out of the general taxation, and are thus divided among the producers in the simplest manner. Large quantities of articles are sold by auction, at which the large buyers, that is the companies of Freeland and foreign countries supply their wants. But the single objects needed are as a rule classed according to their quality by the administration of the warehouse, and their price is fixed according to the average amount of expense which their manufacture entails as computed by the Central Statistical Office and the Bank, and this amount of expense is by no means unchangeable, but as often as demand begins to exceed supply, it is proportionately raised, and in the opposite case it is proportionately lowered.

As we were going through the furniture department of the warehouse where thousands and hundreds of thousands of various pieces of furniture were arranged on view and exhibited with price tickets attached, we observed a figure standing before an artistically made cabinet and wrapped in deep thought, and we immediately recognized Professor Tenax, our former teacher of political economy, to which study we had both devoted two sessions during our technical education at the university of our native place. We joyfully greeted this profoundly learned man who had been much loved by all his pupils, and wished to ask him what brought him here, and how long he intended stopping in Freeland, but he curtly avoided informing us on this point, and exclaimed angrily, " And this is what they call the 'Land of Liberty.' Look here, young people, this is what it must come to if the principles of science are violated. This wonderful piece of furniture which is worth a good fifty pounds in Europe, must be crowded up here with all kinds of miserable market wares and be given away at twenty-five pounds. Is it not the death of special skill if the producers are thus compelled to let their productions be valued according to the incalculable and uncontrollable caprice of an all powerful upper court?"

"But, my respected teacher," objected Charles shyly, " no one compels those who made this cabinet to submit to the valuation which the managers of the warehouse make. If they do not think that this valuation is enough, and they think they can get more, they are quite at liberty to fix upon as large a price as they please. If they are contented with twenty-five pounds for a piece of furniture which would of course have been priced at twice as much in Europe, it means that they do everything here with machinery which is generally done by hand labor in Europe. You will also find that other furniture is proportionately cheap. The price fixed upon by the managers of the warehouse evidently corresponds to the real value of the piece of furniture."

It was the peculiarity of our esteemed friend to answer a refutation which he was unable to rebut by asking a new question, and so he said now, with a disdainful shrug of his shoulders, "And perhaps you call it 'Liberty' here because everyone is compelled to be enrolled in a company if he wishes to do any work?"

"No one is compelled to do that," I observed, taking up the conversation in my turn.

"Really?" asked Professor Tenax ironically. "Then tell me, you young wiseacre, who in Freeland throws himself on his own resources and works alone on his own account."

"No one," I replied. But that is so because no one wishes to."

"Wonderful!" said Professor Tenax, scornfully. "No one wishes to show such a desire because no one dares to. Is it not true that the use of every small piece of land and every grant of credit for manufacturing purposes is joined to the condition, that all the world must be entitled to take part in the productive power which is set in motion with the aid of this ground and this credit?"

"Of course," I replied, "but it follows from this that I can see no injustice if a condition is attached to the use of a thing which belongs to the whole world, and the use of which must be accessible to all the world, and that it is not that which hinders anyone from working on his own account. If I found a whimsical person who wished to work for himself alone, all the world would shake its head at him in astonishment, but scarcely anyone would be found who would take part in his folly."

"One does not know everything when one becomes old," exclaimed Professor Tenax. "Working upon one's own account is such an immense folly that no one is to be found in this country of universal reason who would be likely to do it. It is remarkable that we Europeans, during all the thousands of years of our civilization, have seen before us the opposite of that which you have once for all set forth here as the only possibility. Would you tell me whence comes this change in the intention and disposition of men which has so very suddenly entered here?"

"That is no change in the intentions and dispositions of mankind, but one in the outer conditions of existence," answered Charles. "Even abroad everyone would rather manufacture more and better products by working with others than fewer and worse products by working alone, if he only had the means of doing this, that is, the large amount of capital necessary for large production. Here, where this is possible to everyone, his own advantage compels the workman to join a great union because it is only in this union that he can exercise and employ those magnificent labor-saving machines which multiply fourteen or fifteen-fold his productive powers.

Professor Tenax again changed the subject, and, already somewhat provoked, asked if we could justify the fact that manufacturers who had brought their business into a flourishing condition by every conceivable expenditure of industry and skill should be compelled, through the so-called free mobility of labor, to receive any ugly ruffian into their midst who would do them the honour to share in the fruits of their work. "If I do not have the right to choose my fellow-workmen according to my taste, that is not liberty, but the worst kind of slavery."

"Do the workmen of the rest of the world choose their companions according to their taste?" I asked, meeting derision with derision. "I have seen nothing of that in European factories."

"But in Europe the employer, or at least his overseer, has the right to see the people before he engages them."

"Quite so," I said, "but he does not base his choice on their amiability and conversational powers, but only looks to see whether they appear to him to be fit for the work for which they offer themselves or not. Our directors do that too, and the difference only lies in the fact that these directors, who do not decide about admitting anyone, but only as to the manner in which all the working power is spent, are not the commissioners of an employer standing stiffly and coldly superior to workmen but of the workers themselves. We are by no means worse off in this respect than the rest of the world."

"But not much better," growled Professor Tenax, "and yet you boast that you have set up the best State possible."

"I did not know that we had done so," said Charles. "We believe that we have introduced the best possible arrangement corresponding to the needs of mankind at the present time. We leave it to the gods to attain the absolutely best and perfect in itself. As long as men are not angels, and we do not presume to make them such, they will have to endure the necessary consequences of their mistakes. And therefore, if the separate members are not of one heart and mind with the rest in all things, one party must accept the inevitable, without taking upon themselves to injure the rights of the other party for the sake of this perfect harmony which is desired."

"But do you not understand, then," exclaimed Professor Tenax, "that under the circumstances it may be just as intolerable to see oneself chained to persons who, no matter from what ground, are opposed to one?"

"It is only a question what you mean by this being chained to one another. I shall only admit men into my house, family, and business intercourse who are agreeable to me. It is not a question of social intercourse in the factory, but one of production, and in order that this may succeed peaceably, it is sufficient that my neighbor should understand his work, even if he does not in the least understand or sympathize with my opinions or affections. The personality of the workman is so very much in the background before the power of machinery, especially in modern times, that a moderately reasonable discipline is quite sufficient to make all discrepancies which may arise from personal opposition from henceforward impossible. If we wished to usurp the right to keep persons who have no fellow-feeling with us away from our factory, why should we endure them in our towns? The disagreeable habits, views, or dispositions which a man may possess are much more inconvenient to me if I have to share the same dwelling with him than if I had to share the same workshop with him. For only in the dwelling-house do I have to deal with him as a man, and in the latter principally as a producer of goods. If you also, most honored professor, are an enemy to the freedom of joining any company that one pleases, because it can bring us into contact with every 'ugly ruffian,' then you ought to take the field in the first rank against that political freedom which, as I know very well, stands at the head ot the program of that political party of which you are one of the ornaments, namely, the Liberals."

" One cannot get the better of fanatics like you," said Professor Tenax, as he broke off the conversation, which now became disagreeable to him. But this did not prevent him, since he had by nature a good heart, from willingly accepting Charles' invitation to be our guest frequently during his stay in Edendale.

CHAPTER X.

IMPOSSIBILITY OF A CRISIS IN FREELAND.—THE INSURANCE SYSTEM.

I HAD learnt very quickly to understand why the principle of the free mobility of labor, which consists in nothing else than the removal of every obstacle which opposes well considered self-interest, must lead to the harmony of all economical circumstances. To perfectly remove any obscurities which I might have on this point, I consulted the great classical economists, especially Adam Smith, whose doctrine entirely rests on the carrying out of this principle, and who only erred by concluding that political liberty alone could suffice to remove all hindrances that stand in the way of the working of self-interest. Only one thing was not quite clear, and this was the question whether under any circumstances one of those crises, or one of those universal depressions, by which the *bourgeois* world is periodically punished, could under any circumstances take place in Freeland. Equilibrium is established between the various kind of produce in Freeland by the principle which allows any one to join any company that he pleases, and thus enables the workmen to go to the place where the greatest amount of production happens to be taking place. That is, of course, not possible in the rest of the world, for the workmen who live there do not have the power of choosing the places where they work. They must wait until the employers require them. But the employers in the *bourgeois* world have an advantage which, at least, partly replaces the freely exercised self-interest of the workmen of Freeland. If the business is in a bad condition, they dismiss workmen; if it is in a flourishing condition, they take more on; and one might suppose that profits become equal slowly but surely, and in the same manner that they do in Freeland, and that thus all stagnation of trade must be avoided. Since this is not the case, and stagnation and therefore over-production are more and more becoming the rule, I sought a long time in vain for the real explanation of the difference which I saw so clearly, and which an inner voice told me was a necessary result of the system. The overseer of the warehouse brought me on to the right track at a visit which I made to him concerning the business of my company.

When I asked him if an occasional overfilling of the warehouses would not at least cause a temporary stagnation, he answered me by saying, with astonishment—

" If this happened, for what purpose would all the wares that are heaped up here be produced? You of the Edendale Railway Material Manufacturing Company manufacture the machines which you send here, not because it pleases you to expend your labor on iron and steel, but because you wish to pay for your various needs with the produce of the work which you have expended on the machines. The same is the case with the companies that have manufactured the furniture, clothing materials, provisions, etc., that have been sent to the warehouse. They all sell only to buy, and it can therefore only be a question whether just the right things have been manufactured—those things, namely, which the sellers, who at the same time become buyers, demand. Our liberty of joining any company helps to bring this to pass. It would be necessary, in order that more should be produced than is required, that our producers should not work to enjoy, but only for the sake of working."

And when I further objected that all that also comes to pass in the *bourgeois* world, and in spite of this over-production is always the rule there, the overseer of the warehouse laughed and said—

" You overlook the fact that it is not exactly the same in the rest of the world. There the people do indeed work not to torment themselves but to enjoy; but however much more they produce, they cannot on that account enjoy much more, because the produce of the work does not belong to them, that is, to the workmen, but to a minority, who are the employers."

"Quite right," I answered, "but these last wish to enjoy what the others have produced?"

"No; these few only partly wish for, and only partly can enjoy, what the rest produce. They only partly can do so, because their means of consumption are limited, and they only partly wish to spend it on enjoyment, because they prefer to spend another part of the produce which belongs to them in such a way as to increase their power, and not on enjoyment."

"You think," I asked, "that the employers wish to capitalize part of the produce of the work? Capitalizing means changing the product of the work into an instrument of fresh work. It does not in the least concern the matter which we are now discussing whether the employers buy lace and fine wines, or machines, factory contrivances and tools; they always wish to buy something else for what they sell. And it should always be considered whether exactly the right things are produced, but not whether the things are demanded in sufficient quantities."

"Yes, if the employers of the *bourgeois* world would or could seek machinery, tools or factory appliances in the markets besides lace and wine, there would be no general disproportion between supply and demand. But it is in this point that the mischief lies. They cannot and will not buy any tools and machines, because they have no use for them; which means no use above a certain very narrowly limited amount. They cannot build any new spinning mills if the demand for the material which is spun does not increase, and they can set up no new boot factories if after as before most men must go about barefooted or in torn boots. Nothing else remains for the employers than to employ their so called savings in buying factories, railways and other undertakings, and therefore to increase the price of these by competition. But if an already existing factory or railway, or titles to the possession of such factory or railway which are brought into circulation, should go up in price, then this will cause no kind of demand in the market. Capitalists generally sell off all the productions which belong to them, but they only spend part of the money so obtained in buying other products which happen to be in the market. This naturally produces the disproportion which one dubs with the name of over-production, and which, if it becomes serious, is called a crisis."

This simple statement made me clear as to the reason why a general disproportion between supply and demand is prevented in this country. Since it doubtless corresponds to a law which is universally valid and which requires that no one should manufacture products for another purpose than that of exchanging something for the money obtained from them, and since there is nothing else here which one can exchange than the products of human work, perpetual equilibrium must prevail. This the great economists have, as is well known, laid down as necessary for the commercial world, without clearly knowing why it did not as a matter of fact take place, although they were always exercising their ingenuity upon it. An inhabitant of Freeland can, if he wishes, lay by or save what he produces in another form, but the form in which he saves it can under no circumstances be other than that which causes some product of human work to be taken from the market. He can never in Freeland change the product of his work into a means of power or into a mortgaged claim upon the product of the future work of other men, and can therefore never disturb the equilibrium of the Freeland market when he seeks to acquire such a title to power over others in exchange for his products instead of the products of another. As long as there is a foreign country with respect to Freeland, it may be that those who save money in Freeland place it out in foreign interest bearing investments, but that can naturally only make a disproportion between offer and demand in the foreign markets, and not in the markets of Freeland; for in this case it is the products of Freeland which are exchanged for a title to the possession of foreign goods, and demand of course decreases in Freeland, but so also does supply.

Just as little can foreign commerce disturb the equilibrium

between supply and demand in Freeland. Since it is clear that foreign countries give us nothing, but always exchange goods for goods, there is necessarily a demand for the sale of foreign goods in Freeland corresponding to the proceeds of wares which we sell abroad. Foreign commerce merely enables us to supply our needs of such goods as are produced cheaper abroad than in Freeland, not directly by manufacturing these things ourselves, but by manufacturing instead of them such things as can be made here more advantageously than abroad, and this naturally leads to the result that we can supply this part of our needs much better and more abundantly than as if we produced these articles in question through our own means. On the other hand, it cannot be denied that this commercial intercourse with foreign countries which are visited by frequent and violent fluctuations of production calls forth a greater fluctuation in equilibrium of domestic supply and demand than if we confined our commerce to our own territory. It happens sometimes that a foreign country undersells here with its own manufactures those which we produce ourselves, and the natural result of this is that our own prices, and with them the returns of our production, are lowered; but such disproportions are light, thanks to our power of joining what company we please, and are overcome without much damage to those interested. If we kept aloof from foreign countries, we could defend ourselves against such fluctuations; but as this would be effected at the cost of our international division of labor and consequently at the cost of our prosperity (since we should in this case be always compelled to produce those things of which we are in immediate need, instead of those things which we produce with the greatest advantage), no one in this country consents to uphold such measures of exclusion.

An altogether peculiar manner of laying by what is produced by present work for future use takes place by means of the insurances which are effected by the Central Bank. As I have already related, every inhabitant of Freeland has a right to be maintained by the State when he is unfit for work. This claim to maintenance amounts to four-tenths of the average Freeland income for men, and three-tenths for women, and is sufficient for a respectable and even rich subsistence, but does not under all circumstances enable the recipients to continue unchanged that mode of life to which they have been accustomed during the period of their activity. The insurance department offers to those who wish to have more than the ordinary maintenance amount for themselves and their wives in the later years of their life the means of obtaining this. Whoever pays a premium graduated according to his age can raise the amount of his maintenance to what he pleases.

The peculiarity of this mode of insurance consists in the fact that no interest is given on the premiums which have been paid; the account is also not made in gold, but in the value of work. The following will explain this. European or American insurance companies pay, for example, fifty pounds per annum to a man of a certain age who has paid twenty-five pounds per annum up to a previously fixed time. But the Freeland Insurance Office pays such a man an annual income of the value of two hundred hours' labor for the value of every hundred hours' labor which he has paid every year until he becomes unfit for work. The value of an hour's work in Freeland is about five shillings at the present time, and this would perhaps amount to ten shillings at the commencement of the payment of the proportionate income which we mentioned above, and might go up to twelve shillings before the death of the person entitled to such payments. He would thus have paid an annual premium amounting to from twenty-five to fifty pounds, and have thereby assured to himself an income increasing from one hundred to one hundred and twenty pounds. The object of this arrangement is to make premium and income compatible with lightness of payment on the one hand, and on the other hand with the proportional increase of needs caused by the general wealth. If the value of labor goes up, the incomes paid by the Insurance Office must also go up in the same manner as the claim to maintenance.

Since the Insurance Office of Freeland can of course charge no interest, the increase in the amount of income paid which is caused in such a manner is, strictly speaking, not justified by the principles of insurance. The insured receive on an average really more than corresponds to the amount they paid, and the difference must naturally be borne by the State. But the general opinion in Freeland is that there is no injustice in this matter. The Insurance Office cannot of course make the premiums paid by the insured draw any interest, but it makes them profitable through the means of the Government, whether it is in the form of buildings which serve for the general requirements, or in the form of credit granted to the companies. It is the State which gets the advantage from all these plans, and not only do those who pay premiums and their contemporaries participate in it, but also future generations. Those who are insured have given instruments to the State for doing remunerative work in the present and future out of their savings, and it is not more than just if a part of the increase in the products resulting from the work caused by these payments is presented to them, when the income is calculated, in addition to the amount which they have paid in premiums.

Besides, it must be remarked here that no increasing burden is laid on the State on account of these payments made by the Insurance Office. On the contrary, the proceeds from the insurance premiums enable the amount of capital required by the community to be lent without the common taxation being obliged to reach that height which would otherwise be necessary for getting the amount demanded. The payment of premiums at such a time far exceeds the outgo, and that will continue as long as, in consequence, firstly of the newness of this institution, and secondly of the rapid increase of the population, the number of insured persons who pay premiums is four times as great as that of those who receive payments. It will be different later on, but when this happens, the produce of labor in Freeland will in the meantime have been so greatly increased by the coöperation of the capital contributed by those who are insured that a general raising of the rate will be easily borne.

Finally, I will mention that the whole of the arrangement relates entirely to old age pensions, and not to the maintenance of children. The inalienable claim of the latter to the enjoyment of their share of the general wealth is enough under all circumstances. The Freelanders think it absurd that the future should be encumbered for the benefit of those who have done nothing in the past. Everyone can dispose of the produce of his own labor just as he pleases during his life ; and at his death he is also at liberty to leave what he saves to his children, but no more.

CHAPTER XI.

A HOLIDAY JOURNEY IN FREELAND. DISTRIBUTION OF LAND AND CAPITAL.

SINCE Charles had bespoken the month of August for his holidays—the customary two months of holidays were not, as a rule, all taken at once, but at two different times—I determined to get my leave at the same time. It is also generally the custom that the younger members should consider the wishes of the elder ones when the holiday times are fixed so that the latter have the choice, and the younger ones only have their leave when the elder ones have returned. There is no compulsion in this matter, but I soon perceived that customs and usages have a power here that makes them equal to the severest laws. It is moreover not a peculiarity of Freeland, but a practice which, even if not carried out to such a degree, the rest of the world has made where the greatest proportion of liberty possible has in general come into being. I should not have been able to get away in August, which was the favorite month for holidays, if one of the older members had not of his own free will withdrawn his right out of regard for my friendship with Charles, and had taken September, which had fallen to my lot, as his holiday month instead.

The inhabitants of Freeland chiefly spend their holidays in traveling about. They explore the mountainous region of Kenia, or the Aberdeen range which is seventy chiliometers to the west of this, and enterprising tourists extend their excursions to the mountain chain of Elgon which lies three hundred and fifty chiliometers to the north-west and which shows no single summit which is equal to the Kenia or approaches to it in vastness, but its separate heights likewise project into the regions of snow which begin here, on the equator, at a height of fourteen thousand feet above the level of the sea. Others extend through Uganda to the lake of Ukerewe, whose shores, which lie at a height of four thousand feet above the level of the sea, afford a very agreeable residence and opportunities for excellent sailing and rowing. All the excursions are made very easy by the network of roads and railways, which is still only in its infancy, but which would be a very well developed one according to European ideas. Various building companies of Freeland have erected hotels and villas at the places which are best situated and afford the finest prospect, and a traveler can obtain shelter on cheapest terms either in an idyllic solitude, or among large parties of tourists, according to his taste.

Since the carriage of persons on railways throughout Freeland costs nothing, but like the post, telegraph, and electric power, is provided by the state free of expense, and is therefore paid for out of the general taxation, traveling is in reality scarcely more expensive than living in a fixed place of abode. One gets a conveniently fitted up hotel room for five or at most eight pence, and a whole villa containing from three to eight sitting rooms for from fifteen to forty shillings a week. Provisions are to be had at a fabulously cheap rate everywhere, and only the preparation of dishes in the villas situated in secluded spots costs somewhat more. I have not spent more than eleven pounds during our month's travels from Kenia to Ukerewe, and not three-quarters of this sum was spent on the necessaries of life, but in paying for guides, rowing boats, a sailing yacht, riding horses, etc. If we three, namely, Charles, his wife, and I, had not undertaken the expensive excursion by ourselves, but with a great party, I should have saved half of this sum, and if I had limited myself in expenses of shelter and food, a quarter of this sum would have been sufficient.

No express assurance is necessary to inform the reader that besides the surpassing beauties of the natural lakes the management of the various industries of Freeland interested me very much, and especially the agricultural companies, of which there were only two small ones, in the immediate neighborhood of Edendale, which principally carried on the vegetable and fruit industries. The universal employment of machinery in agriculture as in all works in Freeland is most wonderful. The Company of the Upper Tana now precedes all the other companies in this respect, for it has not more than two thousand four hundred workmen constantly employed on its six hundred square chiliometers or thirty thousand hecatares, and these are of course aided in the sowing and reaping times by from five thousand to ten thousand additional workmen who came from the surrounding companies. And it must not be supposed that the method of conducting the agricultural operations is a superficial one founded upon an irrational impoverishing of the land. On the contrary, the ground is tilled with the greatest care, far more carefully and thoroughly than in any other part of the world, with the exception perhaps of China, but it is the elements which, forced into the service of man, do ninety-nine parts out of a hundred of the work. A magnificent system of irrigation continually gives a rich dampness to the ground from sowing time to the harvest, so that failures in the crops are almost entirely unknown. The plowing, sowing, harrowing, rolling, cutting, binding, thrashing, winnowing, and the storage of wheat, are all done by machines worked by electricity. Numerous spun ropes pass through the fields in all directions, and this net of ropes not only serves for drawing loads, but also for moving and working the machines which are driven by electricity. It is only possible in this manner that one and a-half million metercentner of corn, and besides on an average a million metercentner of other agricultural products, which were all worth about five million pounds sterling, are produced twice a year with an expenditure of not quite thirteen million hours of work. A single hour's work of this kind corresponds to a total profit of eight shillings, and, after deducting payments of capital and the tax to the State, it corresponds to a net profit of nearly five shillings.

We inspected the organization of the Upper Tana on our journey home, and had a meeting there with Professor Tenax, who, indifferent to the beauties of nature, had declined to accompany us on our excursion to the mountains and the great lake. He was so preoccupied when we saw him that he scarcely answered our usual greetings, and one could see by the expression of his countenance that quite a crowd of new thoughts and objections must have risen in his mind during his wanderings among the various factories in Freeland during the last few weeks. Mrs. Vera, who had quickly taken to liking Professor Tenax on account of his great learning and harmless generosity in all questions which did not touch his orthodox principles, nevertheless amused herself at times by exciting him to an extreme display of all his subtlety and dialectical tricks by appearing to take his part. When he therefore greeted us with the ironical question as to whether we had come here to make good our right to the ground of Freeland, and, as we did not immediately understand this, added mockingly, " Here the ground belongs to everyone ; you are evidently here to begin a law suit with the Upper Tana because it has not hitherto allowed you to share in its proceeds," Mrs. Vera interrupted him with feigned sorrow, saying that it had always put her brain on the rack to know what this could mean, seeing that the ground is free as the air, and that everyone could make use of it as it pleased him.

" That is utter nonsense, my dear Madam," replied the Professor with earnestness, "one can give away air to all the world because it can be had in unlimited abundance, but not the ground, of which there is in any case less than corresponds to the requirements of mankind ; and even were it to be had in unlimited abundance, some allotments would give rise to dispute on account of their inferiority, if everyone was allowed to seek for the best piece just as he pleased."

" Professor," I replied, " do you really think that we all want to become cultivators of the soil ? Can I draw plans and guide the plow at the same time ? I stick to my business, although I doubtless possess the right to have my share in the use of the ground, because I find that I make more money there, and this is so because there is a greater demand for the produce of my work at the drawing board than for my work behind the plow. Exactly the same is the case with regard to all those workmen of Freeland who get better wages for their work if they do some other work than that of tilling the ground. And there must naturally always be a great number of these, because human needs are not confined to the products of the ground alone, and so there will always be a demand for what is produced by other kinds of work. The apprehension that all the world would really make use of the right of tilling the ground would only have had any foundation if one supposed that it is of no importance for the people to produce manufactured goods and to find consumers, but that there is a general passion for agricultural labor, a kind of greediness after land which does not regard the result of the work, but only its kind."

"Then what is the use of our so-called common ownership of the soil? What do you and Charles and Mrs. Vera gain by being able to till the ground if you wish to, since, as you have just explained to me, your own interest compels you to make no use of it. Is it not exactly the same, as regards the immense majority of the population of Freeland, whether the land belongs to two thousand land owners or to two hundred thousand agricultural workmen?"

"If the land of this country 'belonged' to the people who till it, you would, of course, be right. Then it would be pretty much the same to all the others, whether those who have sequestrated the earth are many or few. But do not forget this fact. We who stand here have exactly the same right to use the land as the workmen who actually exercise the right of using it. The ground does not belong to the latter; they dare not forbid us to use it if we wish to, and the result of this is that they must divide the advantage of using it with us, and therefore that our work must yield the same profit as theirs, since, as long as this was not the case, labor would emigrate from all the other sources o production to agriculture. Therefore, the right which everyone in Freeland has to possess land does not caus everyone to go in for agriculture, but keeps the profits c agriculture in equilibrium with those of all the other pr ductive employments."

"You have not yet told me," continued Professor Tena "what mystic motive induces a part of the agricultur laborers of Freeland to prefer inferior pieces of ground whilst perhaps other people close by work on better pieces."

"The motive which induces them to do this has nothing mystical about it," replied Charles. "Its name is Self-Interest. You yourself have taught us that the produce of the labor expended in Freeland is proportionately smaller the greater the amount of labor one expends on the ground. Two hundred workmen, for example, will not produce twice as much from a piece of ground which has been given to them as one hundred would, but perhaps only one and a half times as much, because the labor which the second hundred performs is not so necessary as that of the first. If too much labor flocks to the better piece of ground, each single workman would get less produce for his labor from the better piece of ground than he would from the inferior piece less stocked with labor, even if the better ground were ten times more rich, fruitful and favorable. But the self-interest of the workman does not require that he should convert his labor into money upon the richest possible ground, but with the greatest possible profit. It is therefore clear that you only have to let the people choose freely in order that that should happen quite of its own accord which corresponds uniformly with economic reason and justice, namely, that the labor should be distributed in such a manner over all pieces of land, whether they are good or bad, that every workmen gets the same profit."

Our stubborn adversary, flattered by the appeal to his own doctrine, could not withhold a nod of assent, but roused up by Mrs. Vera's roguery, he immediately took new courage to ask in a tone of triumph what would happen if other workmen wished to grow cotton here, where, for example, coffee was grown, and who could prevent the first new arrivals that came from rooting up the coffee trees and thus destroying the fruit of a year's work performed by others? "Has your Land of Liberty also a panacea against such transgressions of unrestrained self-interest?"

"Of course," replied Charles. "Before all I would ask you to perceive that you are not quite clear about the precedent which must be subverted if such a change in the cultivation took place. The first arrivals that happen to come do not have the right to rule and dispose here as they please; but this right belongs under all circumstances to the majority of all those who wish to till the land of this company. A new majority must be formed in order that what you fear should happen. But this is only to explain that it is not the accidental caprice of the first that comes, who might also be a fool, upon which the method of using the surface of the ground depends in Freeland. Without mentioning this last consideration, it does not remain quite the same in essence whether there are many or few who have to resolve upon such an innovation, for in all cases it can only be determined under the supposition that the advantages of all those who have shares in it are taken into consideration. Whoever enters the economy of this association has his share in all its burdens and advantages, and if he then roots up the coffee shrubs and plants cotton in their place, he can only do this if the need of cotton culture is so great as to make up for the damage caused by the destruction of the coffee shrubs. But in this case it is to the advantage of the workmen who were employed there before that such a rational change of culture should take place. If we suppose that a hundred thousand hours of work had been employed on those coffee shrubs which are destroyed, and that the cotton plantations which take their place likewise claim one hundred thousand hours of work, the profit from the new cotton culture would have to be divided among two hundred thousand hours of work, and from this it follows that the coffee trees will only be replaced by cotton shrubs when the latter will compensate, not only for the labor employed in planting them, but also for that expended in planting the destroyed coffee trees."

"And what if it is quite a different branch of industry for which the ground is claimed?" asked Professor Tenax. "If, for example, it is necessary to build factories here on the land of the agricultural company of the Upper Tana, who would decide whether the agricultural company must consent or not?"

"In this case also," answered Charles, "the parallel interests of both parties give the decision in this matter, that is, the interests of the agricultural and manufacturing workmen. Since it is a necessary result of the power which inhabitants of Freeland possess of joining any company that they please that the products of labor should be in equilibrium everywhere, it is quite impossible that workmen who work in factories could wish to erect a factory in a place where damage would be done to other workmen if ground were claimed which had been previously set apart for other purposes, and this damage would be greater than the advantage which the other workmen get by setting up a factory in their midst. The usefulness and advantage of every undertaking find expression in the profits, and these profits are the same for all workmen, as a result of the free mobility of labor. So it is not possible that the workmen of a factory which might perhaps be built here would get the average amount of pay which is usual in the country if the average earnings of neighboring workers were injuriously effected. Consequently no one can set up a factory in his own interests where this must happen to the detriment of his neighbors. There are, as a matter of fact, not less than seventeen great factories in the district of the Upper Tana, which justly claim a considerable part of the surface of the ground as their share. But you may be quite sure that all these factories were only erected because the damage which they did to the agricultural companies by claiming the ground is more than counterbalanced by other advantages. These other advantages can be of many different kinds ; they consist partly in the increased number of consumers that the agricultural company gets for its produce, partly for the reason that it has neighbors whom it employs for improving, driving, or renewing its machinery, but chiefly in the fact that there is an easier opportunity at the time of rest among the agricultural laborers for advantageously converting into money their own, and at times excessive, working power, while conversely the severe temporary need for agricultural laborers at seed and harvest times can be easily supplied by the addition of laborers from the surrounding factories. In a word, the erection of such a factory must be an advantage for the agricultural company of the Upper Tana, or else it would not be erected there."

"But," asked the Professor, who was driven into a corner, "there must still be someone who has to decide whether profit or loss is to be apprehended. Who is this someone?"

"This someone is a majority which is composed of those interested on both sides, and, therefore, of the agricultural and manufacturing workmen. With regard to this I wish you to observe that when such a majority is formed the laborers of the new works on the one hand and those of the old works on the other hand are not opposed to one another as two separate parties. That would only be the case if the advantage of the one went hand in hand with the injury of the other. Since this is not so, and profit and loss on both sides depend upon the same circumstances, interests can never clash here, but only differences of opinion. Part of the agricultural community will think that the erection of the new factory is an advantage, while another part will think that it is a detriment, and in the same manner there will be factory workmen who think that the factory should be erected in this place and others who have the contrary opinion. The majority which is formed in this manner may be mistaken, but their intention always must and will be to do what is equally advantageous for both parties. And if you examine impartially the peculiar meaning of the right to the soil of Freeland it must be quite clear to you that it cannot possibly be otherwise. For since the advantage which is derived from any method of using the land is equally divided among all, thanks to our power of joining any company that we please, it can never be a question for whose advantage the land ought to be used, but only as to what manner of using it conduces best to the advantage of all. The land belongs in every case to everyone. Under all circumstances we are in the condition of partners who carry on their business for their joint advantage, and who may therefore have difference of opinion in single cases as to which method of carrying on the business corresponds best to the general advantage, but never as to whether the advantage of this or that partner should precede or follow that of the rest. I repeat that there are plenty of differences of opinion with us regarding the best method of using the ground, but no oppositions of interests."

"Finally you maintain just the same thing with reference to the distribution of capital! It is a matter of indifference to you inhabitants of Freeland who receives the capital which has been contributed by you? For the capital which your state divides among the various associations comes from a tax to which everyone must contribute, no matter whether he wishes to or not, or whether he needs capital or has an excess of it. Thus one is compelled to save money here, and under some circumstances to save for advantage of others. Is that also just?"

"That would be very unjust," replied Charles, "but it does not happen. Nobody is compelled to save, and everybody contributes only as much capital as he needs himself, and if he does not need any he need not contribute any. For the taxes in which the share of the loan of capital is of course contained are not laid upon the workmen, but upon the produce of the work; only those who work pay for it, and every workman exactly in the proportion of the amount of work that he does. I could, for example, pay three times as many taxes as that agricultural laborer yonder, but only on the ground that my work produces three times as much as his does, and consequently because I get three times as much advantage from the use of the capital."

"Infatuated man!" exclaimed Professor Tenax. "It is not the capital to which you contribute that you draw your advantage from, and it is not the capital to which that agricultural laborer contributes that he draws his advantage from. Perhaps you pay for him, or he pays for you. I have heard that you people of the First Edendale Engine and Railway Material Manufacturing Company are just about to build to the value of three quarters of a million pounds sterling; what does this agricultural laborer get from that? And yet it is his tax as well as yours that must contribute to lend your company this sum. That is an injustice which it is not possible to keep going in the long run without the most hateful coercion."

"That agricultural laborer," explained Charles, "has contributed just as much of the three quarters of a million pounds which our company is using as I have, and therefore it follows as a matter of course that the work which he does is exactly as much as that which I do. I have supposed that that man gets one third of the income which I get from my work, and therefore contributes to our project one third of the amount which I contribute, and it is as clear as day that the advantage which he gets from the plan is one third of mine. Our principle of the free mobility of labor effects this, and its application leads either to a fall in the price of machinery in consequence of our increased supply, or to a rise in the price of provisions as a result of the increase of the means of intercourse effected by us, or to an increase in the amount they produce, or perhaps only to our plans preventing a fall in the profits of the work which would otherwise take place. The final advantage is in all cases distributed uniformly among all the Freeland workmen, and so it is true that a dispute can never arise in Freeland as to who must have the advantage of using a certain tract of land, just as it is true that there can never be a dispute as to who shall have a certain amount of capital, but only as to which mode of using it is most advantageous to all. Capital is just the same thing here as the common property in land, it belongs to all the workmen under all circumstances, and yon agricultural laborer therefore profits by the buildings and machines which we erect just as much as I profit by the granaries and machines which we see before our eyes in the district of the Upper Tana."

"I will not contest this point with you any further," growled the professor, "but tell me this since you have an answer for everything—With what right do you forbid the people here to lay out as they please the capital which they might have saved all by themselves?"

"Who forbids them to do that?" I asked, as I took up the conversation. "There is no one here who would grant to anyone possessing capital what you understand by its advantageous employment, namely interest. No one will prevent you from asking as high interest as you wish for, but it is certain that no Freelander will give either high or low interest for the very simple reason that he can always get capital without interest from the state. To satisfy what you call in this case justice one must compel the people to pay interest, and that Freeland does not of course do."

"Does any one do it in Europe?" exclaimed Professor Tenax excitedly. "Such bad reasoning shows, in my opinion, nothing else than feebleness of your case. Interest is the production of an entirely free proportion of supply and demand, and to see compulsion in this shows either infatuation or an evil disposition."

"If it is as our worthy professor says," replied Mrs. Vera, "I can only concede the point. If the workmen of Europe prefer to pay interest for the use of capital belonging to other people instead of using their own, I consider it is unjust to speak of compulsion."

"Those people," explained Tenax to his cunning friend, "who in Europe use the capital of other people, do not do this out of preference for strange capital, but because they have none of their own."

"Are not those improvident spendthrifts and prodigals who lavish everything that they earn, or idlers who will work at nothing, whilst the others whom they ask for capital are economical and industrious?"

"That is not quite correct, fair lady," explained the Professor, who now began to perceive that his friend had, quite innocently, as he believed, enticed him on to the ice, bnt who was yet too honorable and too prudent to answer immediately to the question in the affirmative. "There are, indeed, prodigals, idlers and drunkards among those who have no capital, just as there are economical and industrious people among those who have capital. But one cannot in general say that this difference explains what we are now talking about. I will even admit that our rich, on an average, consume more and work less than the poor. But ——"

"Strange, very strange," exclaimed Mrs. Vera, with an astonished look. "How does it come to pass, then, that these are poor and those are rich?"

"Now, you must know that the poor have nothing more than their ability to work, and this is unproductive by itself, whilst that which is necessary to make it productive belongs to the rich. Consequently they have the right to require a share of the profits from the poor, because they afford them the means of working; and this share of the profits which accumulates in their hands is that which makes them rich whilst the others must remain poor."

"Yes, I understand that, Professor. Those are poor because they have nothing, and these are rich because they have much. That is quite clear to me. But you must excuse the dull ideas of a woman who has left her beloved Europe in her earliest youth, and can no longer see her way exactly in its customs and principles of justice. Is it not true that the rich have the advantage over the poor in having the means of work, that is, fields and meadows, buildings, machinery, and tools? Has God made the fields and meadows in Europe only for the rich who have made houses, machines, and tools, because they are more prudent, and who now require payment for the use of all this by those people who, on account of their wickedness, have been prevented from possessing the earth, and who are, moreover, foolish enough to produce only the means of subsistence, and not the instruments of labor?"

The Professor was now quite aware of what Mrs. Vera was trying to do with him, and therefore began to be vexed. "What you say is altogether unscientific, my worthy lady," he said. "It has nothing to do with the matter in hand whether God makes a difference between the rich and the poor, and whether it is the poor who produced the appliances for work as well as the necessaries of life. Somebody must still possess the earth and the appliances for doing work, and that somebody is the rich."

"Professor, Professor!" said Mrs. Vera, who now laid aside her jesting mien, and looked full at Tenax with her large clear eyes. "You are moving in a vicious circle; you explain bondage by poverty and poverty by bondage. If it is just that the workmen should not have the profit because they have none of the appliances for working with, and if they do not possess these because they must relinquish the profits, then one must think that it follows as a matter of course that the profit belongs to them if they possess the appliances for work, and that these belong to them if they keep the profits for themselves. Or has the thought of liberty and equal rights something so terrible to you that you must resist it in defiance of all logic?"

The Professor became scarlet, and answered in almost a whisper, with lowered eyes, "You must not judge an old man if he is reluctant to shake off convictions which he has received during the course of a whole life of study. Must I so easily determine to throw away as ridiculous what I, an old man, have commended to thousands and hundreds of thousands of youths as the quintessence of the highest wisdom? The change comes upon me too suddenly. It is antagonistic to my ideas of the necessity of the organic historical evolution of all human things. One does not make a new order of society as a new machine is made in a workshop, and I cannot believe in this Freeland because it is a creation of art and the work of men who are united especially for the purpose of managing the matter so and not otherwise, whilst my experience of the world teaches me that only that which has been organically produced can be reasonable and lasting."

"This opinion is the only remaining entrenchment of your prejudice," answered the young wife inflexibly. "It is, of course, right that new social institutions should not be artificially made, but organically evolved, in order to be reasonable and lasting; but what instrument shall the genius of humanity use if it will change an antiquated form of society, which is on the point of falling to pieces, into a new form fit for existence, except mankind itself? Do you understand by the natural process of creation in the history of the evolution of the human race only such forms as are set in motion without the aid of mankind. Shall stupidity alone, which may produce thoughtlessness, and patiently bears what happens to-day because it is the same as what happened yesterday, shall that be the single privileged force in human history? I understand the theory of the necessity of the organic evolution of the new arrangement of society to mean that the new arrangement must be the natural and reasonable product of the changed condition of the existence of mankind. But this result must, notwithstanding, be brought to pass by men. It does not grow like the trees of the forest or the flowers of the meadow, any more than the institutions of the *bourgeois* world came into existence and were strengthened without the aid of mankind. Or perhaps you think that it is a necessary requisite of a prosperous new building up of society that it should be saturated with blood or rung in with the thunder of cannon? Only resist for the future that which unbiased reflexion and sound manly reason demands from you, and you will not escape a baptism of fire and blood in the *bourgeois* world. But we do not think what we have created to be less fit to survive because it was brought about by peaceful means, and if, in order to make this possible, we sought districts where want of understanding and evil wishes could not hinder us, we have only done what energetic and determined men have done for millenniums under the same circumstances, of which the foundation of the United States of North America stands recorded in history as the last grand example."

Professor Tenax had listened in deep silence to the last part of this severe lecture which was poured over his head. After a pause, he extended his hand to all of us, drew Mrs. Vera's arm under his own, and we took the road to the railway station of the Upper Tana to get into the train which was going to Edendale.

CHAPTER XII.

FOUNDING A NEW COMPANY IN FREELAND.

ANYONE who wishes to have land and capital from the State for carrying an undertaking into effect must make all his wishes and intentions known to the Central Bank, whether he is alone in the undertaking or has already formed partners. The Central Bank publishes the communication made to it, and thereupon calls a general assembly, in which everyone who is in any way interested in the undertaking takes part. A printed declaration was now issued, setting forth that an engineer who had lately arrived from America with some associates who had joined him, partly in America and partly in Freeland, asked six hundred thousand pounds sterling for the purpose of founding a company for navigating the air. His idea was declared to be impracticable by various learned societies of Europe and America, and the governmental department of Freeland, which had to do with undertakings of public utility, together with the board of representatives belonging to it, had declined the project which had been laid before them. He was thereupon thrown on his own resources, and had published a detailed description of his invention, and invited those who, like himself, believed in the possibility of a practical realization of his plans, to join him.

The matter interested me, as much because I wished to see how on this occasion the organization of Freeland would test the merits of an undertaking thus hazarded, as on account of its mechanical nature.

The idea of the inventor was ingenious, but all its details

were not quite clear to me, and in the face of the large amount demanded for the experiment, I found it quite intelligible that our government shunned the responsibility of granting such a sum from the funds of the state. On the other hand I did not think it more than just that an opportunity should be offered to the man for testing his ideas with the aid of public opinion, and I was determined to take part in the experiment myself.

I found nearly two thousand persons present at the general meeting, and all of them had the right of voting by merely being present. Whilst there is no kind of difference at all the other assemblies between those who take part in them, it is a principle at those assemblies connected with founding new companies that those who wish to take upon themselves the risk of the scheme should expressly declare that they are ready to do so. Their vote does not on that account have greater weight than that of the other members of the general assembly, but this rule is necessary, that public opinion, which is interested in the subject, and which is represented by the other members of the general assembly, should determine what security for the credit demanded the State will get under all circumstances to cover the loss in case the undertaking should be abandoned before it has been put in working order or a sufficient number of people have joined it. For by section 6 of the statute relating to companies in Freeland, the loss is equitably divided among the members of every company according to the amount of profit which everyone gets. If an undertaking fails before its profits have been distributed, or if this distribution should have taken place among such a small number of persons that those who suffered loss were not in the condition to make compensation, the State would have found out to its vexation that the undertaking had not as a matter of fact been placed in working order at the expense of the enterprisers but at the expense of the community. Such a precaution is the more necessary, as it is a principle of getting credit in Freeland that no one can be bound to make a higher annual payment to the State on account of a loss of capital than corresponds to the value of an hour's work done every day for a year. Or, in other words, a charge on account of a debt cannot be imposed upon anyone exceeding the value of a daily payment equal to the wages obtained for an hour's work. Since the average value of an hour's work amounts to five shillings at the present time, and there are two hundred and fifty working days in the year—the two months holidays and the public holidays being deducted from the three hundred and sixty days—the maximum payment on account to which an inhabitant of Freeland is liable for the loss of the capital which was lent to him amounts to sixty-two pounds ten shillings per annum.

It is also necessary in founding a new company that a number of members corresponding to the capital demanded should declare at the commencement that they will be responsible to the State for the repayment of the sums demanded, without regard to the question whether a loss arising later on may be paid or not through the shares in the profits which the members obtain. This responsibility is of course extinguished, just as their share of the loss is extinguished, according to the meaning of section 6 of the statutes relating to companies, without charging any of those liable with more than the value of an hour's work per diem for a year.

Since it was a question in the present case concerning £600,000, which ought to be liquidated in twenty years, according to the nature of the enterprise, 240 members had to declare themselves willing to join the undertaking in order that there might be full security for the sum required from the beginning. This did not, as a matter of fact, take place, only 85 persons came forward who either possessed so much confidence in the feasibility of the scheme or who felt so much enthusiasm for the ideas upon which it was founded as to expose themselves to the danger of being burdened with a compensation debt amounting to £62 10s. per annum for twenty years. The undertaking also had numerous and energetic opponents in the assembly, and these proved that the plan was both practically and theoretically absurd in every detail, and that it would be the most foolish waste of public money to expend it in realizing a chimera of that kind. "If," said the opponents, "240 fools had been found to spend their energy on the matter, one must, indeed, pity them, but could provide nothing against it, since it is naturally everyone's right to do what he pleased with his own means. Since this had luckily not happened the inventor can not tempt the public with his chimera any more in the future." I could not agree with this view of the matter in every detail in spite of the fact that it was defended by very able specialists. As I have already confessed, I was in some doubts as to the correctness of all the suppositions of the inventor, but I did not give the preference to the convincing demonstrations of those who opposed the scheme, and I remembered that it was a band of professors who compelled Galileo to retract, and had declared that Fulton, the inventor of the steamboat, was a fool. I was of the opinion that the magnificence of the idea was quite worthy of the attempt in such a rich State as Freeland, and felt myself so much the more strengthened in this idea when I saw that there were some men among the eighty-five partners of the inventor whose judgment in matters relating to aerial navigation was at least worthy of respect. I did not only join the founders, but when it came to a division I joined those who voted that, in spite of the absence of security for capital, the company should receive the credit it asked for; and it was the majority that expressed itself of this opinion.

The result of such a determination is, according to the laws of Freeland, that the matter should come next before the administration and the body of representatives who had to deal with matters of general utility, and it must be understood that this only happens when, as in the case before us, it is a question of founding a company which has not given full security for the amount of capital which it requires, otherwise the matter would have been finished with a decree of the general assembly obliging the Central Bank to grant the required credit immediately. But as the matter stands in this case, the chosen representatives of the State must explain the determination taken by the general assembly. If they agree to it, the founding is accomplished; if they do not agree to it, the founders have the right to demand a fresh general assembly, in which public opinion gives its final judgment. The latter happened in the case before us. The body of representatives for affairs of public interest decided against granting the credit required in consequence of the opinion given to it by the administration, and a new general assembly was called. In the meantime the number of responsible partners of the inventor had augmented to 152, and the general assembly, consisting of 8,000 persons, ratified with an overpowering majority the decree of its predecessor. It was clear that the people of Freeland wished to risk something that such a magnificent discovery might be tested, and I will only mention here that the result was in accordance with the votes of the people. The idea of the inventor did not turn out to be as practical as he had supposed. His undertaking failed, but the experience obtained by making the attempt was so important and of such a decisive nature, that the same body of representatives which had wished to hinder the trial a few months before unanimously adopted a proposal to pay the whole costs and to continue the experiments already begun at the cost of the State, and the inventor, who was for a short time treated by his partners as a queer and insane fellow, was made director of these important experiments.

Our friend Tenax, who was becoming more and more of a Freelander, and took part as much as possible in all public affairs, yet without ceasing his arguments against all Freeland arrangements, had been present with me at the second general assembly, and had voted eagerly against the inventor at the first and with him at the second. When I asked his motives for acting thus, he observed that he had originally considered the man to be only a swindler who wished to get £600,000 out of the Central Bank, and then abscond. "For that," he exclaimed, "is one of the sore points of your credit system. You have considered everything except that there are rascals in the world, and these I would obstruct as much as possible."

"Be tranquil, Professor," I said consolingly to the old gentleman. "Rascals have nothing to do with our bank."

"Oho!" exclaimed Professor Tenax; "does not everyone here get money in what quantities and for what purposes he requires it without the Central Bank having the right to see how the debtor spends the money?"

"Under all circumstances, my worthy friend, everyone gets, as you have just had an opportunity of seeing, only so much credit as he can reasonably pay back. If he asks for more, our administration has the right to examine his purpose more minutely, and the person concerned must behave in a very crafty manner if he can thoroughly deceive the administration as well as the public. If anyone wishes for a greater sum, he must seek for partners, and besides, everyone has the right to become his partner in all cases. These partners watch over him, examine everything he does, place colleagues by his side in the management, which is in itself enough to thwart the criminal plans of an individual. But let us suppose a case in which some one founds a whole gang of swindlers, and that the 152, for example, who have joined the inventor, are polished and refined rogues. But of what advantage is this to them? They have now a credit amounting to £600,000, but for what purpose can they use it, and in what manner? Do you believe that the Central Bank pays them £600,000 over the counter? The Central Bank will pay the building company that is going to erect the factories for the air navigation company and the machine factories which will provide the outfit. Where is there any opportunity for fraud? I admit that they may perhaps give orders for machines in a foreign country, and by this means, through underhand dealings with dishonest manufacturers, could secretly commit some fraud of this kind. But they would scarcely be able to do this even if they used the greatest secrecy, without incurring public suspicion, which would naturally put a speedy end to their game without any interference on the part of the State. But let us look into the nature of the whole affair. If we suppose that they managed it in such a sly manner that no one discovered their tricks in spite of the fact that they had purloined a considerable part of the credit—from whom do they purloin it? Only from themselves; they will not be able to steal more than the amount for which they are answerable. Or perhaps you think that the swindlers, if they have made a good haul, could abscond, in which case the State would have to bear the loss in spite of responsibility of the enterprisers? Do you think that there could possibly be any men who are insane enough to leave Freeland and to hand themselves over to life in the rest of the world for the sake of so much gain? The matter resolves itself into a simple example in arithmetic. What can people steal here? At the most the value of an hour's work a day; and would they for that renounce the value of five or six hours of work a day? For since they leave Freeland they have altogether lost this value, or, at least, reduced it to that measure of misery which is the lot of workmen in the rest of the world. Men who could do this would not be cunning, but blockheads, and such are not dangerous, at least as impostors. But I deny that even the worst blockhead, as long as there is only a spark of humanity remaining in him, would exchange the prison air of the *bourgeois* world for the free atmosphere of Freeland at whatever price the latter were to be had."

"Now do not excite yourself again," said Professor Tenax benevolently. "If it pleases you, I admit that my fears for this tendency have been excessive. The gentlemen of the Aerial Navigation Company are not swindlers, but, nevertheless, they are quite unpractical people. Remember that I am still a professor and have never had anything to do with business myself, but to enter into such a danger as did the 152, and in doing so not to reserve the smallest benefit for myself, and to hold open to all the world the right to take part equally in the project which I have made possible by staking my means, would not be to my taste. I will also observe, besides, that I do not think that there is any evidence of the love of justice prevailing here when one looks upon such a division of risk and gain as something which follows as a matter of course."

"I can also set you at ease upon this point," I replied. "Have you not perceived that that section of the statutes relating to companies, in which the additional payments made to older members are generally mentioned, was left vacant in the parallel statute of the Aerial Navigation Company?"

"Of course I have, and that is exactly what I find so thoroughly foolish. They renounce the insignificant additional payment which the older members of the company enjoy everywhere, whilst I would arrange that here, where so much risk is connected with the undertaking, the first enterprisers should have a greater advantage than the additional payments made on account of age in other companies."

"That is what we promoters of the Aerial Navigation Company think, and we have on that account left the point unsettled. We do not yet know what we ought to demand, and have therefore thought it best to be silent about this for a time. If the undertaking succeeds, a decision is given on the importance and amount of the right of making an additional payment contained in one of the statutes, and then we promoters come forward with our claims."

"And do you call that practical and reasonable? This general assembly which met to-day, at which there was no one except the promoters who would actually take part in the undertaking, would vote for any additional payment on account of age that you liked to ask for. After the space of a year, if the undertaking has succeeded by that time, and if it is proved that thousands of workmen find profitable work here, it is then, at any rate, very imprudent to negotiate with those workmen as to the amount granted when they grant anything to the first 152 at their own cost."

"This question has also taken me some moments to consider, but the answer lies tolerably near. On the one hand it would have been no advantage to us projectors if the first general assembly, which established the company, had granted us some additional payment, because every subsequent assembly can revoke it. On the other hand, we need not fear that later general assemblies, in which the members have the power of deciding, will cut us short in what public opinion thinks to be a suitable recompense, because in that case the power of joining any company that one pleases assists us. Thousands have been found here who help to establish a company in which they are interested at the first opportunity which is offered, and in the same manner thousands would certainly he ready later on to take their part in a general assembly where the just claims of persons who by staking their means have rendered possible the realization of an idea which is advantageous to everyone might be undervalued. Suppose that the flying machines about to be made have actually succeeded in principle, but are yet so formed that they will not be of much practical use, the remuneration of the promoters will remain an insignificant amount, and even a proportionately higher additional payment will not bring in much. Or, supposing the reverse case, that tens of thousands of workmen are necessary to supply the demand for this flying apparatus, not only in Freeland but in the whole world, then an insignificant additional payment would have an enormous value. Let us now suppose the case that anyone, reckoning on a moderate sale, would at this present time consider an additional payment of ten pro cent. to the projectors through, let us say, twenty years, to be just, and it was then proved that this additional payment of ten pro cent., instead of bringing in a few hundred pounds a year, reaches tens of thousands of pounds a year, do you believe that it would be just to reward these 152 persons with £10,000 a year, because, even if the matter came to the worst, they only risked £62 10s. a year? It would be quite as unjust if, in the converse case, one had fixed that this additional payment should be very moderate on the supposition that the sale would be very great, and then it turned out that it is in reality a beggarly amount which is quite out of all proportion to the risk undertaken. We projectors do very well in relying on public opinion, and we shall receive in all cases what it thinks to be just."

CHAPTER XIII.

THE CONSTITUTION AND TAXATION OF FREELAND.

THE various bodies of representatives are chosen in September. The government of Freeland is so constituted that every branch of the public service meets in one of the principal central places. But the various branches of the administration work quite independently of one another, and are not under the superintendence of a single, but of separate representative bodies. There are twelve such branches of the administration which attend to the following departments of public service:—

1.—The Presidency.
2.—Pensions.
3.—Education.
4.—Art and Science.
5.—Statistics.
6.—Roads and Means of Communication.
7.—Post and Telegraph.
8.—Foreign Affairs.
9.—The Warehouse.
10.—The Central Bank.
11.—Undertakings of General Utility.
12.—Health and Justice.

Speaking generally, there are twelve principal executive departments with a director at the head of each, and twelve bodies of representatives from which the directors are chosen who in their turn nominate the subordinate officials.

Every inhabitant of Freeland, whether man or woman,

who is of full age, has the right of voting for all the representative bodies, but only a few make use of this right in the case of all the representative bodies, for most people only vote for those in which they are interested and which they think they understand. Women, for example, do not, as a rule, trouble themselves much about voting for directors of the Warehouse, the Central Bank, the road making and means of communication, the post and telegraph departments, whilst, for example, they generally give the preponderating votes in matters connected with education. People do not guide their actions here upon the principle that it is everyone's duty to trouble about public matters, but only about those in which he is interested or which he understands. It is thought to be unbecoming to hold aloof from public life, but just as unbecoming to mix oneself up in matters which one does not understand. The result of this is that all public matters are in the hands of able men, and that almost everywhere those give the preponderating votes who are most interested in the matters in question.

That would be a great misfortune if it were the case in the rest of the world, for since everyone there strives and must strive to seek his own advantage at the expense of others, such a division of power as this would mean that the public would be handed over in a defenceless condition to those who wish for plunder and are at all able to enrich themselves at its expense. Just imagine in a European State the manufacturers possessing the power of making and watching over the observance of laws regarding manufacturers, the agriculturalists regarding agriculture, and bankers regarding the banking business without having any reason to fear the opposition of those who are not directly concerned in these matters! Here in Freeland such desire for plunder is quite inconceivable. Of what advantage would it be, for example, to manufacturing or agricultural companies in Freeland if they increased the price of their goods by protective duties? By doing this they would have made production difficult for others, and have turned labor from branches of industry which naturally afforded the greatest amount of production to those which afforded less without being able to keep the special advantage of the protected produce for themselves. Since everyone's advantage must be the same as that of everyone else, the protection of the common advantage in every matter can be handed over to those who understand best what is their advantage on any occasion that may arise, and such people are naturally those who are immediately interested in the matter in question. Let us suppose, for instance, the case in which the building of a new railway in Europe is being discussed. Would it be possible there to make the building of this depend on the opinion of those whose lands and factories will be close to the new line? They would vote for building the line even if the advantages which the State gets from it under no circumstances corresponded to the cost, as long as the increased expense which they themselves suffer from building this railway does not exceed the increased advantage. In Freeland, on the contrary, those who are not interested in an immediate manner could not wish that a railway should be made which gives less profit to the State than it costs, because here the profits and costs are equally divided among the citizens, to everyone according to the amount of work which he does, and the single difference between those whom it principally profits, and the rest of the inhabitants of Freeland, only consists in this, that the first are in the best position for deciding upon and estimating the advantage of the enterprise in question. Hence it follows that at the elections here there can never be a desire to help a certain political party to victory, but only to choose men who thoroughly understand the matter in hand. There can, therefore, be differences of opinion concerning the abilities of the various candidates for a vacant office, but never oppositions of interests or party fights. It also happens in Freeland that one person thinks advantageous what another thinks injurious, but it is always concerning what is good for both that these differences of opinion arise, and both parties must therefore always agree in wishing to put the decision into the hands of those who are the most prudent and well-informed and who understand the subject better than others.

The exercise of the right of voting in Freeland is not made conditional upon a long residence there. I was already a voter although I had not yet been quite four months in the country. But since the candidates for the other representative bodies were still unknown to me on account of my recent arrival, I limited myself to voting for the candidates for the departments connected with making roads and other means of communication, and that for undertakings of public utility, because I was acquainted with them. I will mention in passing that the first body of representatives has 120 and the latter 146 members, for the twelve bodies of representatives generally vary in the number of members of which they are composed. They all hold their sittings apart from one another, and their sessions are not all of the same duration. The twelve chiefs of the representative bodies consult together on the more important matters, but they each represent the assemblies to which they belong, yet these also have the right to demand general consultations, which generally happens if one body of representatives is interested in matters which are being discussed by another. Since the constant wish of any body of representatives is always in favor of such a common course of action as subjects the matter in question to the unanimous decision of both or all of those interested, if there should happen to be more bodies of representatives who express such a wish with relation to the same matter, quarrels between the leader's of representatives about encroaching upon one another's rights are unknown. The presidential body decides questions which may arise upon this point.

It will strike the foreigner with regard to the administrative department of Freeland that those two great sources of expense to governments which, in Europe, claim the greatest energy and attention of the State, namely, the finance and military departments, do not appear to be represented at all.

As regards the ministers of finance, of which there are none in Freeland, their place is supplied by the Central Bank in the most effective manner. It is this institution which has the incomes of all the inhabitants of the land in its own hands; therefore no tax collectors are required to collect the taxes. It is sufficient with regard to this matter if the Central Bank debits the taxes to the ratepayers and credits them to the State.

The absence of a war office must not be explained by supposing that Freeland takes no military precautions for making it secure from attack from without. The inhabitants of Freeland have now an army, and, as I believe, a fine one, in spite of the fact that the population does not exceed two and a half millions, a very formidable army, which could easily destroy even the mightiest enemy which might attempt to seize their country. It is not the war department, but, strange as it may appear to foreigners, the education department which has to do with the army. The improvement of every kind of physical fitness, and with it skill in the use of arms, has a prominent place in the education of youths with us as among the ancient Greeks. Beginning at the intermediate schools, the boys and girls of Freeland are exercised daily in magnificent gymnasia, built especially for this purpose, in gymnastics, swimming, riding, boxing, and shooting, for at least two hours, and the youths of the technical high schools are exercised in serving artillery. If the reader now remembers that there are no proletariate here, who are enervated and degenerated, but that every youth of Freeland can develope the full powers of all his faculties, mental as well as physical, and pictures to himself to what perfection such a race would attain on account of its system of practising from youth upwards, he will believe me if I assure him that the marksmen, troopers, and artillerymen which these schools turn out are superior to those of the best European armies in the same measure as the youths of the Greek gymnasia were superior to the barbarian hordes of Persia. I naturally had no opportunity of seeing the inhabitants of Freeland in a real battle, for the State had hitherto been relieved from the necessity of engaging in wars, but I saw them at their sham fights, where, as a rule, they shoot with rapid loading at targets which are ingeniously made and are generally movable. I could also observe the effect of single discharges and volleys, and I boldly hazard the assertion that no European troops could stand against such fire even for a few minutes.

The youths who are too old for school possess a volunteer organization which is conducted by leaders chosen by themselves, and these hold great divisional and general maneuvers every year, in which single warriors and whole battalions, amounting to a thousand, contend for various prizes. These consist in nothing else than simple branches of laurel which are not on that account less eagerly sought for than the olive branch at the Isthmian games of the old Greeks. I witnessed such a fight, and declare that the victorious thousand to which the prize was awarded received it for making 6780 hits with ten volleys delivered in one minute at the distance of a thousand meters. I know quite well that there is a difference between shooting at defenceless wooden targets, which, I may remark in passing, were exactly of the size of a man, and at an enemy which returns the fire. But neither is it necessary that a thousand men should shoot down six or seven times as many to make themselves absolutely unapproachable by every human enemy. And if anyone thinks that the result is incredible, he may also consider that in the course of history up to the present time the fully-developed man has always snatched away the victory from degenerated slaves, even if the proportion of numbers was as unequal as this. It was not the military genius of Miltiades that decided the day at Marathon, nor that of Pausanius at Plataeæ, but the invincible dexterity in the use of weapons which the Greeks who had been brought up in the gymnasia of Athens and Sparta possessed against the helpless hordes of Asiatic slaves. What wonder is there if the youths of the gymnasia of Freeland would now oppose a similar superiority to those hordes which the rest of the world might send against them.

I have yet to explain why the superintendence of health and justice is given to the same body of representatives. In the first place, this shows a small estimation for the care of justice, which is put down everywhere in the rest of the world as the principle of social order, and as such thought worthy of special care. The differences lie in the fact that in this country justice lies in the general organization, and that one does not accordingly find it necessary to enforce it by special mechanism. The *bourgeois* world, which rests on injustice, since it compels nine-tenths of its men to sacrifice their own advantage, or what they hold to be such, to that of the State, must naturally devise minute provisions in order that it may thus subject to the command of the State those compelled to abandon their own advantage. No one in Freeland is compelled to do what is to his disadvantage, or to abandon anything which is beneficial to him; here the advantage of the State stands in perfect harmony with everyone's peculiar interests, and it is superfluous to defend these interests of the State, surrounded by the insurmountable wall of general self-interest, through special safeguards. We also have absolutely no police here, and no courts in the European sense of the word. Disputes occur occasionally, but these are settled by arbitrators who exercise their office voluntarily and gratis. There are also criminals in Freeland, but we generally look at these as mentally or morally ill, and deal with them as such, that is, we do not punish them, but seek to improve them. And it is physicians and not judges to whose care the conduct and superintendence of the process of improvement is entrusted. The latter is the reason why the administration of justice goes hand in hand with the superintendence of health. For this reason it must be perceived that such dealing with those who are mentally or morally ill gives little trouble in Freeland, since there are proportionately only a few who must be submitted to it.

There is nothing wonderful in this; the inhabitants of Freeland are a long way off being angels. It is indeed to be hoped in a not too remote period, and at any rate after the course of some generations, that the want of almost all provocation to actions at law will call forth a beneficial change both in the disposition and in the nature of the people. Just in the same way as organs of the body which are not continually used must wear away, the same is the case with the organs of the soul's existence. Even the worst man, in so far at least as he is in a sane state of mind, does not do evil without a cause, and even the best man can commit a crime, if the provocation to do this becomes too powerful; but it is not on that account less true that good as well as evil actions have an influence on the character of a man; evil actions make him evil, and good actions good. It is to be expected that the men of this country, where there is no cause to do evil, must always become better and better. But a long space of time will have to elapse before this improvement in the disposition of character is accomplished, and sometimes, I repeat, I cannot acknowledge that the inhabitants of Freeland are better men according to their innermost hearts, than our fellow men in other countries. Nevertheless, I maintain that the very rare occurrence of crime here is nothing wonderful. Do the inhabitants of foreign countries murder, steal, and commit fraud out of pure villainy, and because it pleases them to do so? They do it, at least ninety-nine times out of a hundred only from necessity or temptation. Now, there is no necessity or temptation here, and, therefore there is no cause for ninety-nine crimes out of a hundred which are committed abroad, and that is the reason why they are not committed here.

This absence of necessity and temptation is of course not to be understood as if the difference between Freeland and foreign countries only consisted in the fact that the people here are satisfied, whilst there they are hungry. Even the satisfied people in the rest of the world commit enough crimes—not so frequently, however, as the hungry—but they do it because they find themselves as it were in a continual state of war with all their fellow men, and because one is naturally not so exact about right and wrong in war as in peace and among good comrades. It is well-known that there is a kind of honor amongst the most abandoned, and amongst the swindlers and bandits of the *bourgeois* world, which is nothing else than the aversion to injure anyone who they think is unwilling to hurt them, and who is therefore confident that they will respect his right. If the inhabitants of Freeland also respect each other's rights without exception, one could almost maintain that in this point they do almost nothing else than what, without regarding diminishing exceptions, the most abandoned in Europe do in similar circumstances, they spare their confederates. And the difference only lies in the fact that the inhabitants of Freeland are all confederates, whilst those belonging to the rest of the world, as a general rule, look upon and treat each other as enemies.

After I had given my vote for the two elections which interested me, I determined, being conducted by Charles, to take a view of the other voting places which were in the same building, namely, the People's Palace, in order that I might observe what happened in them.

When we entered the session hall of the body of representatives for the Central Bank of Freeland, where the assembly of this particular elective body used to meet, angry cries met us, and we perceived that the crowd was collected around an orator whose performances evidently called forth this disturbance. On approaching nearer, we saw our friend Tenax, who, as I should mention, had told us a few days before that he intended, in spite of the manifold crimes of the commonwealth of Freeland, to settle down altogether in our midst, and he was here publicly making his first attempt to contribute his mite for the improvement of one of these shortcomings. As such he was exposing to his temporary hearers, as we were soon convinced, the exorbitant amount of the taxes of Freeland.

"Freeland," he exclaimed "desires to know nothing of ground rent and interest on capital, but if you have to pay a tax of thirty-five pro cent. on your income, rent and interest are included in it, and you are in a worse plight in this respect than the people abroad, who do not on the average have to pay more than from four to five pro cent. under both heads, and for both together, if they reach high amounts, ten pro cent."

To the great surprise of our professor, this striking argument altogether failed to have its expected effect, but rather occasioned hilarity. A few of the members of the assembly did indeed desire to take the matter tragically, and to worry themselves about the affirmation of our friend, but it was some of those who had very lately arrived from abroad, and they were soon quieted by the majority of the old inhabitants, who explained to them that everyone must be permitted to express his opinion freely here.

When the Professor perceived the unexpectedy poor results of his speech, his embarrasment was so great that one of those present, apparently with the intention of sparing their strange guest the abashment caused by no one's thinking his explanation worth answering, replied in a short speech.

"Friends," he said, "this man evidently has quite honest intentions towards us, and it is not is not his fault if, with his head yet full of the confusions which are bred in the outer world, he cannot tell black from white in the country. Perhaps his eyes will open if I remind him of two things. Firstly, that in foreign countries ground rent and interest on capital are paid out of the amount of the capital, whilst here the tax is taken out of the income. I have worked in a factory in a foreign country, and I perfectly remember that the five pro cent. interest on the capital employed in it amounted on an average during a year to exactly as much as all the wages of the workmen, managers, and overseers employed there. My father also was the head servant of a farmer who had to pay annually twice as much farm rent as the total amount of wages which he paid. The second thing that I would say to him, and that in my opinion is the principal point, is that the interest in foreign countries belongs to other people, and is spent by them for their advantage, whilst the taxes in Freeland belong to us, and are spent up to the last farthing for our benefit. It does not only concern me how much I pay, but also from what and for what I pay it. When I was abroad, I was a poor wretch who must part with the last and much needed farthing in order to enrich others; here I am a rich man who pays so that he may become yet more rich. And our new friend has actually forgotten this difference."

Only he can measure the abashment of our good Professor who knows how much the instruction they give from the chair, and which therefore may not be called in question, has become second nature to most teachers. He unmistakably received the reproof contained in the lecture imparted to him into his inmost mind: so we did not disturb him when, without taking leave of us, he silently lost himself in the crowd.

CHAPTER XIV.

SOCIETY, LOVE AND RELIGION IN FREELAND.

THE two rainy seasons, the longer of which ends in July and the shorter in October, are festivals in Freeland. It must not be supposed that these rainy seasons are periods during which rain is always pouring down any more than that the dry seasons are periods of uninterrupted drought. There is rain in Africa during the whole of the year as well as fine weather, but in the rainy seasons there is more rain, and in the dry seasons less, than at ordinary times. However, the contrast prevails to the fullest extent only in the equatorial lowlands, whilst the mountainous and alpine regions of Kenia and its immediate neighborhood have similar climatic conditions to those of the temperate zone. But whilst copious showers fall almost daily during both periods, there is also regularity even in this. The mornings are generally clear and fine, but towards the afternoon thicker and thicker clouds collect about the summit of Kenia and descend in the form of thunderstorms during the evening and generally half of the night, and Europeans hardly have any idea of their violence. The nights during this period are totally unfit for remaining in the open air, and the Freelanders have to arrange their pleasures accordingly.

Whilst it is customary to use the balmy nights of the fine weather, as far as they are not devoted to sleep, for excursions and all other kinds of amusements in the open air, the people generally amuse themselves during the rainy weather in covered halls, and in these dancing holds a prominent position. Every place in Freeland has one or several committees of amusements which arrange public balls, and families which have grown-up daughters regularly meet at these in friendly circles for the pleasure of dancing. But it must not by any means be imagined that these public and private balls are the same as those of Europe. People do not assemble here to rival one another in dress and to calumniate one another, but exclusively for the sake of pleasure and without any other designs.

Jewels are unknown here, not perhaps because the men and women of Freeland are altogether without vanity; on the contrary, they value beauty and outside appearance, and the women especially take a good deal of trouble to show off their personal charms advantageously. The inhabitants of Freeland are not in want of the means of manufacturing all kinds of jewels, but they value them little, because the expense of the articles is not in itself sufficient to make them of any more value. It may seem strange, but the Freelanders prefer flowers to jewels as ornaments. At first I conjectured that there was some democratic tendency underlying this, but women with whom I conversed on this subject soon taught me something better.

Everyone will admit that from an impartial esthetical point of view flowers are more beautiful than artistic and costly jewels. If, in spite of this, the latter are valued more highly in Europe, it is because they are more costly, and the possession of costly things gives their owner the credit in the *bourgeois* world of having a high station in life. A jewel is a kind of patent of nobility there and shows that its wearer is not a servant, but a master, and that he has the right of using the work of others for his own advantage, and therefore of selling the happiness and honor of thousands upon thousands to obtain his own title to nobility.

"Do you really believe," said the wife of a director of our factory at one of the Edendale balls, "that diamonds are valued highly because they are pretty? I can assure you that when I was in Europe, I could tell the difference between diamonds and cut glass as little as I can now. But in spite of this, I longed to possess a diamond necklace, whilst I rejected the idea of wearing a necklace of cut-glass with indignation."

"How do you explain that?" I asked.

"I wished less to deck myself out than to be distinguished from other people in some manner. I am quite convinced that if it was the privilege of the upper classes of Europe to wear a nose ring, those women who value a place in society would strive their utmost to obtain the right of wearing one. Now, it is the privilege of the powerful and influential classes of Europe to wear diamonds, because they are dear, and therefore one buys them instead of things which are far more pleasing, useful, and pretty. And if it were just the same thing here, I assure you that I would even wear diamonds here, in spite of the many changes which have taken place in my views and habits. But in Freeland a diamond would not show that I belong to the more influential and powerful classes, but to the more foolish, not that I may employ the labor of others in satisfying my own caprices, but that I employ my own for producing useless and unimportant things instead of those which are useful and agreeable. I should excite pity instead of envy, and that alone you see—that I do not make myself out to be better than I really am—is the reason why I prefer in this country the bouquet in my breast to the most costly brooch, and the roses in my hair to all the stones in the world."

Fashion has lost its tyrannical sway in Freeland for exactly the same reason. Clothes are worn here solely for the two-fold purpose of veiling and embellishing the person. Disfiguring oneself and thereby out-doing others is here considered to be the summit of folly. As a matter of fact, dress in this country, and especially that of women, is extremely beautiful in consequence of the observance of this principle. Very great care is expended upon it, and, as I have learnt, even great painters and sculptors do not disdain to dabble a little in the business of the costumier. But as expense is never a matter of consideration in choosing the material, or newness or rarity in fixing upon the cut, but only excellence of dress, the impression which such a ballroom in Freeland makes when filled with the gracefully moving self-possessed and noble figures can hardly be expressed in words.

But what gives its especial charm to the society of Freeland is the frank childlike joy that beams upon one from every face. One lives here not only among sincere people, who are in a prosperous condition, but, what is more, among people who can reckon with absolute security on the continuation of their prosperous condition. The people of Freeland are not absorbed in the struggle for existence, and everyone here is himself responsible for the greater or less amount of his prosperity. The hateful tormenting anxiety about one's daily bread and the security of economic existence is quite unknown to the inhabitants of Freeland. It is even possible that the company with which one is connected does not do much business and must be dissolved; this may cause loss, but never endanger future prosperity, for it is the inalienable right of every Freelander to make use of the immeasurable riches of the whole country. This pleasant assurance, together with the consciousness that, wherever one may be, he always finds himself among mates, whose advantage is his advantage, and whose detriment is his detriment, gives to the society of this country a sincerity, cordiality, and in particular a security the equal of which is not to be found elsewhere in the world, for there men do not fight with one another for existence but against one another, and there one's neighbor is not one's comrade in the general war against nature, but the enemy against whom self-preservation compels people to defend themselves with all the weapons of cunning and violence.

The idea which is current in Freeland with regard to this difference between social matters here and in the rest of the world is characteristic. "What would you have?" said a Freelander to me the other day with whom I discussed this subject. "We are not better than animals, not even than beasts of prey, but have only ceased to devour one another as those who live in the *bourgeois* world do, and have returned to the morals of beasts. You will say that the tiger eats the ox, and the wolf the lamb. We also do that, but we spare one another. We have not become super-human beings. The truth is that formerly we ranked below the brutes, or, if it sounds less objectionable to you, among the worst of all the brutes."

Since the relations between men are generally so elevating here, it delights me to describe the relations between the two sexes. Nature has planted in every man whose disposition is perfectly sound, a deeply-rooted and mighty pleasure in women, as the highest of all instincts, and in every woman of sound disposition a similar pleasure in man; but in *bourgeois* society this powerful instinct is poisoned. Woman is sentenced to be subjected to man, and man must on his part fear in woman a rebellious slave. The maiden who lives away from Freeland is compelled by circumstances to attract by means of her charms a " supporter " who must make good to her what society promises her, and in her fellow women sees competitors in this unpleasant struggle for future existence. Candor and dignity are consequently excluded in the relations between man and woman just in that first stage where they should be doubly necessary in making choice for the whole future of one's life and where both parties should appear as they really are to prevent them both from suffering any harm. And what is worse still is that in the rest of the world a maiden looks upon a man in the first place as her future supporter, and consequently as a prize to be captured, while conversely every man looks upon every maiden principally as a possible claimant to his future support, and therefore, as a man-hunter trying to capture and out-wit him. Thus there really exists an everlasting condition of distrust, hypocrisy, and suspicion between both sexes.

All that is quite different in Freeland. Here man is to woman and woman to man nothing more than what nature has appointed them to be; a woman stands secure on her own right, she does not need a husband to live, but to love, and will, therefore, only endeavor to conquer where her heart is already conquered itself, or at least longs to be conquered. Men know that, and can give themselves up to the tender passion when they feel inclined to without distrust. Since they are not used, they can be quite sure of not being abused, and since a Freeland maiden is, in the same manner, quite sure that the man who woos her is thinking about her person alone, and not about her means, connexions, or position in society, she will distrust her suitor just as little as he provokes her distrust. And, above all, she does not marry for a price; she does not look upon her suitor as her future supporter, she knows quite well that among the thousands of young men whom she meets, only one can be the chosen one, and she, therefore, waits with tranquillity until the voice of her heart points this chosen one out to her. The relations between the sexes are consequently free from restraint, and therefore quite sincere, and young men and maidens have intercourse with one another simply as companions. But they especially strive after truth and happiness, which in certain relations even exceed the amount customary in Freeland. Marriages in Freeland are not less natural and happy. The married state is, as a matter of fact, extremely steadfast here, and separations hardly ever occur, although marriage, from a legal point of view, rests solely on the free agreement of the parties. Since, as a universal rule, one cannot be compelled to do anything in Freeland which encroaches upon another's rights, and since no right to the person of another is recognized under any circumstances, marriage is considered to be a free contract, which is only made by the agreement of both parties, but which can be immediately dissolved at the wish of one party. There is not even any exception to this rule if there are children from the marriage, for in this case they belong to the mother, unless she agrees to any other arrangement. Since children, for whose protection alone the foolish marriage laws of the rest of the world have been made, are in Freeland either not obliged to be maintained by their parents, or are so only to a small extent, this recognition of the natural right of the mother follows as a matter of course. And it is just as self-evident that this perfect abolition of all compulsion in marriage causes as a matter of fact an unusual steadfastness of marriage in Freeland. This also entirely corresponds to the experience of the rest of the world, where the constancy of the matrimonial tie stands everywhere in inverse, and the frequency of divorce in direct, proportion to the difficulties with which the law invests divorce.

There are no differences of rank in the society of Freeland. This is especially the case with young people who have received their education in this country. Boys and girls are educated together, and receive the same education (which nearly resembles that of the best German middle schools), the former until they are eighteen years old, and the latter until they are sixteen years old. Classics are only taught to those who wish it; in other respects the whole of the youth of Freeland receives a thorough grammar-school education. As soon as this step in their education is finished, they separate to their various professions. Those who devote themselves to higher branches of learning or art go the Universities or to the Academy of Arts, and the others go to the various technological institutes where they receive theoretical and practical instruction in their future crafts. The natural result of this training is that the simplest workman is not only acquainted with the whole working of his trade, from mechanical dexterity to the knowledge of markets and the fluctuation of business, but also possesses a very considerable amount of general culture. These workmen of Freeland are no unthinking, narrow-minded automata, who have no interest in anything but the occupation in which they happen to be engaged. They are always able to criticize the whole of the professional body to which they belong, and this naturally contributes to make the choices of the general assembly wise and reasonable. Besides, they can always utilize a favorable opportunity offered by a business of the same kind as that in which they are engaged, by transferring their labor to it, and this again helps to guarantee the equality of production in all branches of industry in the most perfect manner possible. Finally, they are all cultivated men in the highest sense of the word, and can take part in all human affairs, and show acute understanding of and a lively interest in art, learning, and public life. It does not, of course, follow from this that every workman in Freeland really troubles himself about all the concerns of mankind.

There are many among them who are just as indifferent to what does not touch their own interest as numerous people belonging to the learned professions, for participation in the general culture of mankind does not only depend upon the amount of knowledge, but also on personal dispositions and plans, for where the latter are wanting the former is of no use. It must only be said that the difference of profession in Freeland is not decisive on this point

Just as natural is it that in Freeland every honorable kind of work should be equally esteemed by public opinion. The same thing is usually said in the rest of the world, but it is nothing else than one of the many lies with which the people there are deceived. The *bourgeois* world generally considers it a disgrace to work, and rightly so, too, for there the workman is usually a bondman, a tool for the purposes of others, and dependent upon their will, or, in a word, a slave, and no moral law will make the honor of a slave equal to that of a free and independent man. There are indeed, naturally, various modifications of the ignominy of work in the outside world. The more perfect the wearing out to which the workman is subject, that is, the greater the suffering and the less the pay, the more complete is the disdain. Only those enjoy perfect honor in the outside world who do not work at all, but who let others work for them. Here, where everyone works for himself, and where no one can be misused as a means for the purpose of others, it cannot make any difference whether the workman follows these independent purposes of his in one or the other manner. But this is absolutely impossible in Freeland, because no hard and fast distinction can be drawn between the different professions. The simplest handicraftsman can be advanced to-morrow to the rank of those who work with their brains if he is called to a leading position by the confidence of his comrades. But, besides that, a continual changing takes place from brainwork to handwork, and *vice versâ*, because numerous brainworkers prefer to perform some kind of handwork at certain intervals for longer or shorter periods of time. They do not in the least prejudice themselves by doing this, and get thereby a healthy and, under all circumstances, even agreeable interruption of their sedentary mode of life. I have lately become acquainted with one of the upper officials of the Central Bank, who annually devotes himself to two months of agriculture and gardening. A teacher of my acquaintance works at a factory for some weeks every year. So common is this custom in the whole of Freeland that all offices and bureaus are organized with regard to it, that is, are arranged so that permission can be given to a large number of the employees to make such a temporary change in their profession. It follows, of course, that wages cease during such leave.

The result of this is that differences of profession are not noticed in social intercourse here. A man chooses his associates solely according to their personal qualities, and if it is also natural that those of similar intellectual talents, disposition, and interests prefer one another's company, this has nothing in the least to do with what is called in Europe social position.

Sometimes, of course, the addition of new immigrants who are partly on a lower grade of intellectual development disturbs this general social equality, but this difference decreases gradually every year. The immigrants, with a decreasing small exception, eagerly wish to elevate themselves intellectually, and the welfare as well as the ease which without exception fall to their lot enable them to recover the neglected years of their slavery in a surprisingly short time. Besides, the rising youth which has grown up in Freeland preponderates over the immigrants who are not yet completely absorbed by the State, and it may be safely reckoned that before a generation has passed the equality of rights which already prevails will be completed by a perfect social equality.

In conclusion I will add a few words on the religion of Freeland. This also stands under the influence of the principle of absolute personal liberty and equality of rights. The State presumes just as little to trouble itself about the belief of individuals as it does to direct and watch over their work. As a matter of fact all the great religions have adherents in Freeland, and numbers of them have united themselves into ecclesiastical societies which worship

God according to the dictates of their conscience. The universal culture and enlightenment offer more than sufficient protection against the ministers of the various religions mixing themselves up with the political and social affairs of the State. It must be acknowledged with pride that in other things the priests of this country are without exception free from that desire for power which is the prominent characteristic of their caste in the rest of the world. They are also men who do not forsake the current of thought in the midst of which they perform their duties. In the rest of the world, where true liberty is not recognized, and where everyone has only the choice of ruling or being ruled, they naturally determine, as all others do who are in the same predicament, for the former. Here, where nobody either rules or allows himself to be ruled, it does not occur to them to make an exception. There is, therefore, no known case of the State of Freeland having been annoyed by priestly lust for power or by intolerance. Should any minister entertain a wish of this kind, it could be confidently left to his own congregation to bring him to reason.

CHAPTER XV.

FITNESS OF THE PROFESSIONS WHICH PEOPLE CHOOSE. ART PRODUCTIONS. COMMUNISM AND ANARCHISM. THE ADMINISTRATION. GENERAL PRACTICABILITY OF THE FUNDAMENTAL PRINCIPLES OF FREELAND. FEAR OF OVER-POPULATION.

PROFESSOR TENAX wished to get a professorship of political economy at the Edendale University. He employed some months in inquiring into the agreement of the rightly understood axioms of political economy in every point with the principles of Freeland, and the result of his investigations and reflections was generally a very favorable one. Yet the conscientious man thought it necessary to have a train of thought which he had not yet been able to reason out by himself explained in a deputation with the economists of Freeland. For that reason he offered to have a decisive debate with two Edendale professors of political economy, and allowed me to have the honor of being present during this wordy warfare. It took place at the house of one of the Edendale professors, and the day fixed for the discussion arrived.

"I must first of all remark," said the Professor, as he introduced the discussion, "that I know quite well, with reference to some of my views, that they have, as a matter of fact, been refuted by the manner in which Freeland has been developed up to this time. But I am a theorist and not a practical man, and I wish to know whether what I see here must occur on account of its inner essence, or whether it is only the result of an accident. To begin with what lies nearest to us, I ask what guarantee is there that the self-governing workmen will always seek the most skilful and fit persons for carrying on a business, and not those who wheedle themselves into their favor by loud-sounding words and alluring phrases. They have at least learnt in Europe to place persons at the head of the labor parties who get over difficulties well if they want them to guide those under their leadership to useful production."

"The workmen of the rest of the world," replied one of the Freeland professors, quietly, "are quite right if they do not place skilled men of business, but skilled agitators at their head, for producing does not concern them, but agitating. Just as little as it follows that, because I choose in case of war the most suitable fighting man as leader, I should vote for the same man as rector of our university, even so little can one conclude, because agitating workmen place the most suitable agitators or the most energetic brawlers at their head, that they will think in a similar manner if it concerns the superintendence of their work. Workmen, as a rule, understand their own advantages, and are not so foolish as to overlook the fact that other qualities are necessary for managing a factory than those necessary for leading a political movement or organizing a strike. In other respects freedom takes care that any mistakes that may be made should be repaired very quickly. For a badly managed company becomes prudent by the example of the better managed companies, and if this does not happen with due promptitude, such a company sees itself very rapidly deserted by its members and is obliged to liquidate. That is the struggle for existence, as we understand it, in which the incapable and unfit are necessarily succeeded by those who are better and more fit."

Professor Tenax bowed his assent, and went on to another question, "How is it," he asked, "that labor in Freeland cannot suffer through discontented people and sedition-mongers. There are, as it is well-known, men of genius all over the world who are mistaken in their views, and there are also blockheads everywhere who believe in such men. What happens if such troublesome people emerge here with their followers? Is it not to be feared that they would bring disorder into the best regulated society?"

"Not in the least," was the reply, "We have an irresistible weapon against such mistaken people, and this is nothing else but the free right which everyone has of carrying his ideas into effect. It has, as a matter of fact, repeatedly happened that empty-headed fellows have attempted this, but they have ventured nothing when they had the opportunity of giving effect to their big words. The means of the state were placed at their disposal for this purpose, as well as at that of the existing companies, but of course only as far as they could find helpers for the practical realization of their idea, but they hardly ever found these, so little credit did they have to carry them into execution. If we had wished to compel them to remain sensible, they would have raised a clamor about this violence, and there would have been no end to their plotting. But since it only depends upon themselves to commit some folly, they wisely let it remain, and there is an end of all plotting. Even in this point, freedom has proved to be the best defense of order."

Professor Tenax again gave his assent, and continued, " I can now in the main answer the following doubt for myself, namely, the question whether quarrels are to be expected from the political and especially from the socialistic sects. If anyone, for example, is fanatical about absolute equality, and feels vexed because his manager is paid more for his work than himself, he is quite free, always supposing that he finds partners, to seek for a manager who will be contented with a pay equal to that of five or six hours of work a day. But such attempts could be a source of disturbance if they occurred frequently. How do you explain, my worthy colleagues, that I have not seen such a radical rage for equality anywhere, and that anarchical experiments are just as little cared about in Freeland?"

"We think that that can be explained very simply by assuming that the ideas of absolute equality are nothing less than a hallucination of fever caused by hunger. Men are so evidently equal in capacity and needs, that only a madman could think of enforcing this absolute equality, which is contrary to human nature, if there were no starvation. All men wish for enough, in this point we are, as a matter of fact, all equal, and in a society where foul and brutal misery is the order of the day, it is evident why an equal division should be desired. But if it appears that everyone, if he only has the means of employing his strength can by moderate work not only get necessaries, but also superfluities, and can obtain beautiful and agreeable things, it is no longer a question of dividing bread, but roast meat and confectionery. It would, therefore, of course be folly to wish that every one should receive an equal portion, no matter whether he wants it or not.

"And as concerns anarchism, the endeavor to overthrow, together with authority in the social field, all political order also, this is likewise explained by the hatred towards a particular form of political order which condemns the majority to pay for the progress of the civilization of others with their own privations. Where everyone shares in the fruits of progressive civilization, it occurs to no one to attack that order which must necessarily exist with the progress of civilization."

"Before I proceed to the two principal questions which contain the remainder of my doubts," says Professor Tenax, "I wish to have an incidental question cleared up. This is, whether all imaginable branches of labor are compatible with the principle of allowing anyone to join any company that he pleases. In the first place, how does one observe it in performing artistic work? Must a painter allow any persons who please to force themselves upon him as assistants, and what can he do in this country to keep such unwelcome companions away?"

"The fact that the painter does not need the wealth of the state for his work, defends him from such companions," replied one of the professors, "and therefore the lack of that condition in his case to which the duty of admitting companions to his work is attached. But let us suppose that it is otherwise, and imagine the case in which a painter or sculptor has no place in his own house for his work, and also that the materials for executing it demand so much money that he asks for a loan from the state; he is now obliged to allow anyone who wishes to join him in his work. But do you think that public opinion would endure that his work should be disturbed by unbidden intruders? As soon as the slightest attempt to do this is noticed, the painter only has to call a general assembly, to let this name him manager with full powers, and then either to employ such partners as offer themselves in doing mere handwork, or, if he does not require them, not to use them at all. Should malevolent persons wish to compel him, he always has sufficient votes from his fellow citizens to make an enactment to render such attempts vain. Our supreme mistress, public opinion, does not force itself into anything unasked, and lets everyone do what he likes. She is ready to help at once when any-one's actions injure the rights of others just because she never encroaches unnecessarily or excessively. Injustice can only happen here under the supposition that anyone who is unjustly treated is silent about it."

"I am also satisfied on this point," said Professor Tenax. "Would you now explain to me what means Freeland employs to administer justice in cases where the principle of the free mobility of labor is unable to produce equilibrium in the proceeds of work, or at least where it cannot do this without injuring the economy of production in the highest degree? It is not just that the value of every piece of goods should depend upon the proportionate amount expended upon it or can be made so to depend, and it is unjust because there are goods which are produced by the voluntary activity of nature and not by human labor; goods which mankind does not produce, but only collects. The tree in the forest is not made by the man who fells it, and therefore in the value of the wood the work of the wood-cutter will not be paid for, but the gratis production of nature. The same is the case with the ore of a rich mine in which not only the work of the miner must regularly be paid for, but also the rarity of the product which does not depend upon this. Such a value on account of rarity, which is conditional upon natural cir-cumstances, can indeed occur in the majority of all the branches of production. Now I admit that the liberty of joining any company that one pleases might equalize all profits if driven to to the extreme. If we take mines again as our example, those which are more productive will employ more labor until the share of the profits which a single workman gets is the same everywhere, but under some circumstances that can only take place in such a manner that the work done by single laborers is confined to the more productive mine. This can also be prevented if the more productive mine hands over to the State, or to other mines, the excess of their profits above the average usual in the country, and thus brings about an equalization of the profits. But it appears to me that the people of Freeland do not consider the latter method to be sufficient or the most suitable for every case, for I observe that single workmen, and especially miners and foresters, are taken into the employment of the State. Is there not in this a confession of the deficiency of the principle of the free mobility of labor?"

"Not at all. Just as little as it is detrimental to the principles of private business which exist in the rest of the world if the State itself carries on such business, is it detrimental to the principles of the free mobility of labor if the State itself joins these mining companies. The principle is adhered to in both cases as long as the State does not deviate from them. It would be detrimental to the economic arrangements which exist in the rest of the world if the State should sanction any other than the existing principles in the branches of economy which it carries on, and, just in the same manner, our principles could only be violated if our State wished to smuggle foreign or communistic principles into the businesses carried on by it, or even could do so. It can do this just as little as a foreign State could work according to our principles. From which it appears that the main thing is the system according to which those who work in such State businesses are paid. This consists in the rest of the world in granting the amount of WAGES customary in the country, that is, the amount which is thought necessary for carrying on life, according to the locality and time of year, but with us in granting the full PRODUCE of human labor, which is customary in the land. Just as a *bourgeois* State must pay its employees as much as corresponds to the usual minimum necessary for existence, because otherwise it would not find the necessary amount of labor, and just as it cannot grant any more to them than this minimum amount, because it would otherwise be inundated with demands for work, in the same manner our State must always grant the same full amount of produce from the work to its employees, in whatever branch of the business conducted by it they may be, seeing that other workmen of the country enjoy it, and it cannot grant them more because it would altogether lack the means of stopping the pressure of workmen. In short, our State is excluded from commercial activity as little as other States, but with us, as in the rest of the world, the economy of the State is regulated by the principles upon which society is constructed, which are exploitation there and justice here."

"I come now," said Professor Tenax, "to the first question of principle which I have already mentioned. Do you believe that it is possible to apply the principles which you follow in Freeland to the whole of mankind? If you believe that, do you think it possible that this can happen everywhere while existing rights are respected, and, whether you believe the latter or not, why have you sought out this spot in the interior of Africa for carrying into effect your schemes for rescuing mankind, and have not preferred to achieve them among the civilized nations of Europe or America?"

"The affirmation of the first point of this question follows as a matter of course," was the reply. "Since the maxims of Freeland are entirely founded in human nature, no reasonable ground can be seen why they should not be applied everywhere, and obtain the same result as here in Freeland. For we do not suppose that those who belong to our state really have any more than that very moderate amount of cultivation which is necessary for undertaking what is manifestly to their own advantage. Our workmen need no deeper understanding of economic questions, they have only to understand that it is better to get five shillings than four shillings for the same amount of exertion. Neither do we demand special virtues from men. Freedom and justice have the power of improving men, but it is certainly not necessary that men should be better in order that freedom and justice should be introduced, for freely ruling self-interest and not communism is the leading principle in in Freeland.

"But economic freedom and justice are not only possible everywhere, their victory is unavoidable, otherwise all progress of civilization must have an end. For since human wisdom has succeded in compelling the inexhaustible power of the elements to do work, the plunder of man by man through a cruel, but unavoidable necessity of civilization —as it has been for thousands of years—has become a hindrance to civilization. There is now no more demand for the results of increasing production as long as the working masses remain shut out from the enjoyment of the full value of the proceeds of their work, and since things for which there is no demand cannot be produced because they are worthless, exploitation chokes that wealth as it arises which would immediately be forthcoming if there was any market for it. Servitude has become the sole cause of misery, and since misery is barbarity and powerlessness, it must and will yield to that wealth which signifies civilization and power.

"So our principles not only can, but they must come into effect everywhere. And that may well happen without injury to vested interests. Just as the service imposed upon peasants and the ownership of slaves was peacefully abolished in due time in many states, so that could happen in the case of private property in land and capital. The immeasurable increase of wealth, which would naturally be the result of bringing the powers of production and consumption into equilibrium, would afford the means of doing all these things with the greatest ease, and since the former owners can no longer get interest out of the compensation money which is awarded to them, but could use it solely for gradual consumption, it would not fall heavily upon them to make the payments extend through a long course of years, and by doing this all our burdening of the new economy would be avoided even at the beginning. It is to the interest of the new order of things that, when it is brought into existence, all existing rights should be respected, since such commotions and disturbances should be avoided as are likely to be prejudicial to the future. But in spite of this, we doubt whether the unavoidable transit from the economy of robbery to that of freedom will be accomplished in such a quiet and forbearing manner everywhere, or even in the most civilized state. In order that this should happen, the propertied classes must themselves take in hand the peaceful revolution or at least agree to it, so long as they possess any power at all. And they will probably not do that anywhere. But it is not to be expected that a violent resistance on the part of the rulers would be met with forbearance by a successful revolution. It would probably depend everywhere on the tenacity of the propertied classes whether the new order of things would have more or less regard for their claims. The more obstinately they oppose themselves to the wheel of time, the more certainly and cruelly will they be crushed under it. I also answer the second point of your question at the same time ; the transit to social freedom and justice could take place with the most perfect forbearance to rights already in existence, but in most countries it will take place with only partial or absolutely no observance of these rights and will even result in bloodshed.

"The third point is now essentially answered. The gentleman who puts these questions appears to think that the founders of Freeland should have placed the lever in the midst of *bourgeois* society and taken the risk of bloody resistance being made, because they would in that manner obtain more surely and more quickly the liberation of the disinherited masses of the world, upon which greater importance must be laid than in making an asylum where at the most only a few millions can find room. As a matter of fact, it is the principal purpose which is constantly before us here to liberate all our fellow-men who are groaning under exploitation. But we are convinced that we have done more for the liberation of the world by founding Freeland than if ever so effective an agitation had been made in the states of Europe and America. For since it is quite certain that the propertied classes, who have the power in their own hands everywhere, would have resisted our endeavors, so it is likewise quite certain that we should have been obliged to limit ourselves to agitating whilst here we could act. And the eloquence of what has been done is much more powerful than words which have been ever so well thought out and arranged. Just as those English Independents who laid the foundation stone of the United States of North America in the seventeenth century did a greater service for the political freedom of the world than if they had remained in their English homes and had vainly suffered there for their cause, so do we also believe that we have done more for economic freedom by working here than if we had suffered elsewhere without acting."

"You also almost convince me," said Professor Tenax, "that Freeland is destined to bear its organization over the whole of the world, and that it will attain this, its highest purpose, sooner or later. Then will want and misery take their departure from mankind. Do you believe that that can happen without over-population following as a natural result, and are you not apprehensive that over-population must lead to want and misery again? Malthus has shown that the increase of population is always endeavoring to exceed the amount of space disposable for growing food, and that unlimited increase must be stopped through want of food. Now the economic order of the rest of the world keeps at least a minority of the people from the unavoidable results of want, but if the economic equality of rights becomes generally observed, then, if want supervenes again, it means a general retrogression of civilization into barbarism."

"Malthus has not proved what you have just stated," answered one of the professors of Freeland, "and what is, as a matter of fact, thought by the rest of the world to be an irrefutable dogma, but he only asserts it. And that this assertion, which mocks evident facts and which has been hovering in the air for a century, is received as a demonstrated truth, is only one evidence more of the prejudice and blindness of this remarkable time, which, in its successful efforts to find out the secrets of nature, has altogether lost sight of the great connexion between all natural and human things. It is, of course, true that the multiplication of mankind, as of all other living things, must have some limit, and it is just as true that starvation and privations will, under all conditions, become a limit to the increase of population, but it is untrue that men increase under all circumstances until they are decimated by hunger. Much more does the most superficial glance at the facts show every observer who is not entirely blinded by prejudice that, as a rule, the opposite takes place, that men do not increase, and have not increased, to the limits of the amount of room disposable for growing provisions. Were it otherwise over-population must be the general rule, whereas the earth could, as a matter of fact, easily support a hundred times the present number of human beings. Malthus appeals to nature for the proof of his theorem, and even there the contrary of what he wishes to read out of her takes place. Want does not prevail in matter, but boundless excess; even those species which are the most fruitful increase nowhere, or only in the most isolated exceptions, up to the limits of the amount of room disposable for growing food. That Malthus could get the foolish idea that men do starve, and have always starved, because there are too many of them, and that he was even possessed with the more foolish illusion that the same condition of regular starvation should rule everywhere in nature, is only explained by the fact that he saw starvation as an evident fact among mankind, and could not discover the right explanation of it, namely, that the masses starve because the things which would satisfy them are kept away from them, and on that account availed himself of the expedient which is everywhere adopted where correct explanation is wanting, namely, of setting up a natural law where there is nothing else but an inverted social organization. The truth is that nature possesses a number of means besides starvation for preserving equilibrium in the propagation of every living being. Increase of population would find a limit in starvation if it were not otherwise limited, but as the latter is not the case, since other natural sources produce equilibrium between the means of propagation and mortality long before the limits set by starvation are reached, so can the latter at most produce in an exceptional case the effect ascribed to it by Malthus as generally taking place.

"But the high significance which is attributed to Malthus's doctrine of over-population by the *bourgeois* world would not be justified, even if this theorem in itself rested upon truth.

It is at all events much more certain and indubitable that the coal fields of the earth must be exhausted in a conceivable time, if they are used in the manner in which they have hitherto been used, than that the earth must continue too narrow for mankind if workers had all the means of satisfying their wants. Why does the rest of the world vex itself, not about the exhaustion of the coal mines, but carefully leaves the production of future fuel to future generations, whilst it is constantly racking its brains about the over-population of these same generations? A large amount of conscious or unconscious hypocrisy lies here; one seeks reason for a method of behaving of which one is instinctively convinced that it cannot be justified. The theory of over-population is in truth only put forward for nothing else than for the purpose of justifying the shame of handing over to pitiable misery uncounted millions of fellow creatures who have equal rights with ourselves, whilst we still possess the means of rendering the existence worthy of a human being possible to them."

This interesting exposition ended here. I had not very often seen a professor worsted before, and worsted in a discussion, who would have been so gratified by reason of his defeat as was my once so tenacious teacher and friend Tenax now. On taking his leave, he shook hands with his two successful opponents in such gratified manner as if it only depended upon their good will to render possible, or to hinder his going over to Freeland.

"I have now done with the past," said Professor Tenax as we separated. "My whole future will be occupied in spreading those ideas which I have imbibed here."

CHAPTER XVI.

CONCLUSION.

I NOW close the diary of my experiences in Freeland, and for a very strong reason, because my time, which had hitherto been divided between work, study, and pleasure, is now filled with feelings, thoughts, and actions, moving altogether in one circle, the center of which is a woman who, for me, is the sum total of everything that is noble, beautiful, and good. Or, in other words, I have fallen in love.

The reader need not fear that I shall trouble him with an effusion concerning my love; this concluding chapter will be nothing else than as dry a narrative of a betrothal as there could possibly be. I must only relate one thing more, because it indicates the manner in which the maidens of Freeland think.

When I was engaged to my bride and we began to talk about the arrangements of our future house, I had told her that I had left a very large amount of property in Europe, some of which I was already disposed to give to the State of Freeland, while I thought the rest would be suitable for purchasing the luxury of a fine and agreeably arranged establishment. My bride thereupon blushed, and eagerly begged me to renounce these thoughts. When I asked the reason and desired to know why my intention caused her so much repugnance, she hesitatingly explained to me that it was quite uncomfortable to her to enjoy a luxury which arose out of the privations and misery of her fellow creatures. "I should feel," she said, "'as if I was feasting on human flesh. I, who have breathed the air of Freeland since my youth, can just as little endure to enjoy something which has been produced by hunting human creatures to death through over-work and privations, as a woman who has been brought up in Europe would endure a number of fat men being killed and served up in her house."

And she gained her point. The remainder of my property in Europe, which was "honestly acquired," according to the ideas current there, by my forefathers, lies in the coffers of the governmental department of Freeland which deals with foreign affairs. This employs such payments made by rich citizens, in addition to the means expended by the State for the same purpose, in enabling constantly greater and greater masses of foreign proletarians to emigrate to Freeland.

THE END.

LONDON: WILLIAM REEVES, 185, Fleet Street, E.C.

www.ingramcontent.com/pod-product-compliance
Lightning Source LLC
Chambersburg PA
CBHW020258170426
43202CB00008B/426